Have no fear, Remote Work Is Here!

How To Thrive In A Remote Work Environment

Elbert Holden

Have No Fear, Remote Work Is Here!

© **Copyright 2021 Elbert Holden - All rights reserved.**

The content contained within this book may not be reproduced, duplicated or transmitted without direct written permission from the author or the publisher.

Under no circumstances will any blame or legal responsibility be held against the publisher, or author, for any damages, reparation, or monetary loss due to the information contained within this book. Either directly or indirectly. You are responsible for your own choices, actions, and results.

Legal Notice:

This book is copyright protected. This book is only for personal use. You cannot amend, distribute, sell, use, quote or paraphrase any part, or the content within this book, without the consent of the author or publisher.

Disclaimer Notice:

Please note the information contained within this document is for educational and entertainment purposes only. All effort has been executed to present accurate, up to date, and reliable, complete information. No warranties of any kind are declared or implied. Readers acknowledge that the author is not engaging in the rendering of legal, financial, medical or professional advice. The content within this book has been derived from various sources. Please consult a licensed professional before attempting any techniques outlined in this book.

By reading this document, the reader agrees that under no circumstances is the author responsible for any losses, direct or indirect, which are incurred as a result of the use of the information contained within this document, including, but not limited to, — errors, omissions, or inaccuracies.

About the author

I am a Career Counsellor/Advisor by profession. I have a bachelor's degree in psychology and a master's degree in counselling. Practically, I have been working in this field for seven years and five of those last seven years were remote. As a career counsellor/advisor, I assist clients in assessing their interests, personalities, and abilities to choose and pursue the profession that best matches them. I advise folks who haven't decided on a career path or are unsatisfied with their current one. I spend most of my day as a career counsellor interacting with clients. Early sessions should focus on the client's background and conduct to assist them in better understanding their own motives and desires. With a broad range of experience, it's easy for me to guide a client through the process of researching fields that match their interests, conducting informational interviews with them to supplement their research, and finally targeting or creating specific job positions that meet their needs. I address almost every problem one can probably face related to their careers. Working remotely for such a long span of time has made me experienced enough to walk in the shoes of every remote working employee or employer thus I can understand the problems and hurdles they face and can compute great solutions for them too.

Have No Fear, Remote Work Is Here!

Contents

Chapter 1: Remote work blow-by-blow - 5

Thriving in remote work - 10

Cultural obstacles of remote work – 24

Weighing up the pros and cons of remote work – 31

Chapter 2: Remote work implementation - 43

Setting up a remote team as an employer – 43

Necessary digital tools for remote working - 49

Ensuring the engagement of employees - 59

Remote work challenges for employees - 68

Hiring a remote team - 75

Tips for optimizing Workflow of Remote Teams - 84

Chapter 3: What lies ahead - 89

The future of remote working – 89

Recent operating issues of working from home – 96

Why distributed teams should still meet in person - 98

Going from pandemic remote work to planned remote work - 101

Landing a remote job – 106

Chapter 4: Employee precision – 111

Writing job descriptions for remote workers – 111

KPI'S to measure the performance of remote workers - 122

Giving your employees the right training – 126

VILT training - 131

Tackling disciplinary issues in remote work - 138

Team building tips – 140

Team building activities - 144

How to determine remote workers' salaries - 151

Chapter 5: Making the shift – 159

Convincing your boss to let you work remotely - 159

Misconceptions about remote work - 166

Consider your personality type before going into remote work - 170

Chapter 6: Social media revolution - 182

How hiring managers hire remote workers through social media - 182

How to avoid getting distracted by social media when working remotely - 188

The role of social media in remote working – 191

Chapter 7: Remote communication – 195

How to lay off a remote worker - 195

Managing your inbox whilst working remotely - 198

how to clarify email communications - 201

Managing remote employee performance without seeming cold and distant – 206

Tips on running effective brainstorming sessions remotely – 211

Conclusion - 223

Resources - 225

Have No Fear, Remote Work Is Here!

Introduction

Covid-19's rapid and unprecedented changes have hastened the shift to remote working, requiring the total migration of practically entire enterprises to virtual work in a matter of weeks, leaving managers and staff scrambling to cope. To accommodate their new remote workforce, businesses have been obliged to swiftly improve their digital footprints, using cloud storage, cybersecurity, and device tools. This has become a major issue this year for the majority of businesses and employees.

Due to technology that is increasingly developing virtual workspaces, the "under one roof" approach of conducting business has significantly declined over the last decade. "Move work to the workers, not workers to the workplace," is the new paradigm. Companies see benefits in how remote work expands their talent pool, lowers turnover, decreases real estate costs, and improves their capacity to conduct business across time zones.

Working from home may be rewarding and productive if you develop a strategy that makes use of the benefits of working from home. We finally have a chance to make meaningful decisions about integrating remote and office work and how to make the most of our days at home, after a year in which many of us were thrown into remote work by surprise. Working from home means creating a harmonic work-life balance while increasing productivity and working at the greatest job (not simply one close by).

Have No Fear, Remote Work Is Here!

And those are only a few of the benefits of leaving the office behind. Remote exposes a slew of other advantages, as well as practical advice for easing your way out of the office door, where you have complete control over how your day unfolds. It is believed that employees who can work from anywhere are more productive and engaged. As a result, leaders must be able to lead from any location.

If you're an employer who's stuck with traditional working ideas but wants to keep up with the world and shift your employees to remote work without disrupting your business, or if you're an employee who desperately wants to shift his job to remote work in order to maintain a work-life balance but doesn't know how to do it or is worried if it will work, This book covers all you need to know about remote work, from what it is to how to perform it effectively, as well as its advantages and disadvantages. To make things easier for you, a variety of tools and methods have been discussed. Finally, to make things crystal clear, I've shared a few techniques for doing efficient remote work based on my personal experience of working remotely.

I've been working remotely for the past five years and doing it very efficiently while also managing my tasks. As a result, this book is mainly about my personal experiences. The issues I confronted, the strategies I adopted, the resources that aided me, and the methods by which I discovered solutions. It's essentially my personal experience working remotely; thus, everything in this book is dependable and trustworthy enough to be used by the average person to achieve successful and desirable results.

Have No Fear, Remote Work Is Here!

When I first started working remotely and ran into some troubles, I looked for a few solution guides here and there to see if they could assist, but nothing did, so I opted to fix the issues one by one on my own because we all learn from our mistakes and experiences. That's when I decided that when I had the perfect remote working life, I would publish a book to help someone terrified of failing. Every new endeavor is difficult at first, but those committed to achieving their goals will go to any length to achieve them. The biggest coward is the one who does not even attempt something because they are afraid of failing.

Whether you're a manager trying to figure out how to deal with employees who "want out" or a worker who wants to better your lifestyle while still performing well at work, this book is a must-have.

This book will teach you how to do the following:

- Focus on objectives rather than the 9-to-5 workweek to gain control over how and when you work.

  - Treat your bosses like valued customers to impress them.

  - Prioritize important emails and texts to avoid information overload.

  - Make online meetings more focused, intentional, and engaging.

Have No Fear, Remote Work Is Here!

- Build strong bonds with your coworkers, whether they're on the other side of the office or in another city.

- Strike a balance between working from home and family life.

- Make a remote work strategy that allows you to get the most out of your time at the office—and the most out of your time at home

- And much more!

CHAPTER 1: REMOTE WORK BLOW-BY-BLOW

What exactly is remote working?

As the name implies, remote work entails doing one's job from a physically separate location from the office. While traditional work arrangements require employees to report to an office every day, remote employees work from home, using digital collaboration and communication tools, document sharing, and other features to bring the office to them.

Many of these individuals work remotely from home, but remote work can be done from almost anywhere. While some remote employees opt to work from home regularly, others work from a variety of locations. Remote work can be done in a variety of locations, including:

- Home.

- Coffeehouses.

- Spaces for co-working.

- Hotels.

- Vacation homes for families.

- Public Libraries.

- Any location with a computer and an internet connection.

While some jobs, such as factory labor and retail sales, demand that individuals work in a specific physical place, remote employment has fewer restrictions. People who work remotely may be hired full-time, part-time, on a contract, or a project basis, and the conditions of their contracts may differ.

There are two main remote work models:

1. Permanent remote work.
2. Flexible remote work.

In permanent remote work, a remote worker's full job is completed outside of the office. Everything from paperwork to team meetings and conference calls occurs at the remote employee's home or the preferred location. The remote worker does not need to come into the office because they have access to all the information they need and the tools they need to stay productive from anywhere. Permanently remote employees are frequently part of remote teams, which means that all of their coworkers work from home regularly. Even though such teams may never have met in person, they employ collaboration and communication tools to achieve common goals and instill a sense of team and business culture.

Have No Fear, Remote Work Is Here!

Flexible remote work, also known as hybrid remote work, is a hybrid work arrangement in which an employee is allowed to work from home and has to go into the office on occasion. Some flexible remote work arrangements have established timetables, with individuals working from home on certain days and going into the office on others. Others may have flexible schedules that allow employees to work from home most of the time and come into the office only when necessary, such as to attend client or team meetings. In the United States, 89 percent of companies intend to make flexible remote work a permanent option, allowing any or all employees to work from home at least one day per week.

Why do companies do remote working?

Companies do remote working for the following basic reasons:

- Productivity.
- Performance.
- Profitability.
- Engagement.
- Employee Satisfaction and Retention.

Productivity:

The stereotype of remote employees as slackers who don't have genuine jobs is just that: a myth. On the contrary, telecommuters have been demonstrated to be more productive than individuals who operate in a traditional office setting. Moreover, increased effectiveness among remote employees is connected to the liberty telecommuters have, which leads to fewer workplace interruptions and more flexibility in working hours.

Performance:

Workers generate outcomes with 40% fewer quality faults when they have more autonomy through geographical independence. This is because employees have been given more personal and professional autonomy over their private lives and professions, which means they are more likely to give their best performance. After all, they enjoy what they do.

Profitability:

Some of the costs associated with onsite business operations, such as office space, equipment, and travel reimbursement, can be saved by remote-enabled businesses. For example, part-time telecommuters save an average of $11,000 per year, resulting in a 21 percent increase in profitability.

Engagement:

Telework eliminates hiring borders and leads to more diverse workplaces by removing geographic barriers separating companies from the best candidates for their open positions. Hiring managers may pick, screen, and evaluate individuals in a virtual setting, from advertising job vacancies to accepting applications and conducting interviews. Stronger engagement, or, in other words, 41% decreased absenteeism, results from increased productivity and performance.

Employee Satisfaction and Retention:

According to a Mom Corps online study, telework is one of the most wanted benefits that businesses can provide to job searchers, with 42 percent of employees willing to take a pay loss in exchange for more flexible work alternatives from their employers. Additionally, after a remote work agreement is offered, 54 percent of employees say they would change employment for one that offered them greater flexibility, resulting in a 12 percent drop in attrition.

Have No Fear, Remote Work Is Here!

How has COVID sped up the growth of remote working?

Even before the coronavirus outbreak, an increasing number of people chose to work remotely, and many organizations have adopted more flexible workplace arrangements. According to the Federal Statistical Office data, the number of workers working from home for at least half a day per week increased from 18% to 24% between 2013 and 2018, just before the crisis. However, the recent controversy surrounding Covid-19 may radically alter this. According to another survey, almost half of all employed or self-employed persons work from home during the crisis. Even though the bulk of these people will return to work once things have returned to normal, the number of persons working remotely is unlikely to return to pre-Covid-19 levels. Another survey stated roughly 25% of respondents worked from home at least once a week before the crisis. However, 34% predict that they would be able to work from home at least once a week after the crisis.

How can we thrive in remote work?

When it comes to remote work, there is no one-size-fits-all solution. Everyone works differently. They work at various times throughout the day. Various work locations and Different time zones are involved.

Even if remote work isn't a new trend, many people are still learning how to work from home by trial and error, trying to be happy and productive.

Those who have done remote work before as well as those who are just getting started face hurdles.

And it's not just individuals that struggle to make remote work work; entire corporations do as well.

Best Practices to Thrive as a Remote Worker:

1) Maintain proper meeting etiquette.

It's easy to tell whether someone is checking out during a meeting in person. They fidget with their pen, start reading emails, and possibly fall asleep. When calls are made over the phone, however, it is far more difficult to detect indicators of apathy. So, ensure proper meeting etiquette and pay close attention, so you don't miss vital details and regret it later.

2) Practice with what works best for you.

It's easy to fall into the mindset that you should be able to sit at your home office desk in the morning and work nonstop until the evening. But unfortunately, things can quickly fall apart without the built-in discipline and natural breaks of a workplace.

It's up to you to figure out the ideal approach to work from home. When we work in an office, we go on walks to purchase snacks, talk to coworkers, take coffee and tea breaks, and schedule lunchtime away from our desks. However, at home, these natural actions begin to feel like we're cheating or slacking. As a result, people are now working longer hours with fewer breaks, all from the same location every day. This is almost probably a tragedy waiting to happen, as well as burnout.

Experimenting to find the optimal approach to work is the best way to get out of this trap. Allow yourself to experiment with different start times, work from different locations, and wear various outfits. Your office's temperature, audio setup (headphones, earphones, microphone), the amount of comfort in your chair, and the desk you utilize can all affect your productivity or distraction.

3) Make documentation and clear communication a top priority.

Remote workers' communication dynamics are vastly different from those of people who work together in an office.

The days of walking over to someone's desk whenever you need anything clarified are gone. Suddenly, you're dealing with multiple time zones, as well as Slack and video communication. In addition, working from home necessitates deliberate and well-planned communication. Things may be misconstrued or never communicated if this is not done.

Make a point of documenting more than you normally would. Create documents to outline your ideas and agree on the next steps, for example. Everyone will be on the same page this way.

4) Draw a line between business and personal life.

For remote workers, the lines between work and personal life become increasingly blurred. Because most of us work from home, the work and home/life environments have merged into one never-ending entity. Wake up, check your email, eat breakfast while working, continue working all day, and then it's 10 p.m., and we're still working. This can be incredibly harmful to your health.

Unplugging is crucial. As a remote worker, you'll need to set up boundaries to assist you in separating work from your personal life. Otherwise, you may suffer from burnout, social isolation, and even despair.

5) Make your presence felt at work.

When you work in an office, you are constantly in the public eye. Your employer visits you frequently and inquiries about your projects. People remember you because they run into you all the time, so they invite you to meetings and schedule time to talk with you. In addition, people come up to you at your workstation to say hi. Unfortunately, this is not an option for Remote.

We're relegated to a name on a Slack sidebar outside of meetings. Unless we take steps to make ourselves noticed. Allowing folks to know what you're working on is a simple yet incredibly efficient strategy to stay visible. It's natural for your coworkers — and even your manager – to become engrossed in their daily routines. As a result, it's up to you to remind them of what you're up to (and, frankly, your existence).

There are various strategies to be visible remotely, including using Slack, scheduling meetings with your team members, and sharing papers before and after meetings (like notes and agendas). All of these factors help others on your team remember you.

6) Set aside time to socialize.

You eventually miss out on the built-in social benefits of working in an office when you work remotely, and it's easy to spiral into lunacy unless you set out time and build a social plan to engage with other people in person. As though they were your friends. This is particularly relevant because, contrary to common assumptions, most remote employees are not introverts.

Make sure to participate in any activities you select, whether it's time with friends, gym classes, gatherings, or coffees with individuals from your co-working space. Make a note of them in your calendar. Invite friends to hang out with you. Remove your slippers and force yourself to leave the house.

7) Make friends with your teammates.

Getting to know your coworkers outside of work will make you feel more connected, productive, and satisfied at work. Even if you work primarily alone, feeling a sense of belonging to the team will help you appreciate your work. You may feel alone and even miserable if you don't feel connected to your team.

Don't rush into work when you get a call if you can help it. Instead, spend at least a few minutes catching up on what's going on with everyone. The more you learn about your coworkers, the more satisfied you will be with your decision to work with them. You can even use full meetings to get to know one another and catch up on things that aren't related to work. This can be done with virtual teas/coffees or liquids.

8) Conduct post mortems on important projects.

On a remote team, postmortems are my secret weapon. It's how we finish jobs so that we're ready to tackle whatever comes next. Postmortems also tackle the most difficult aspect of remote work: communication and documentation.

A postmortem is a written report made after a project is completed to evaluate how it went and what should be done better next time.

When a project at FYI is finished, we conduct a postmortem. It could be a new feature we developed, a marketing campaign, or a significant bug.

The person in charge of the initiative is responsible for filling out the postmortem form with all relevant project facts and then gathering feedback from the rest of the team.

9) *Pay attention to your health.*

Working from home can deplete your vitality if you let it. On my way home from work, I used to always go to the gym. It was easy to fall into the positive habit since I had momentum and a routine.

You're at home with the remote, so the temptation is to stay at home. It's easy to work in your pajamas, order takeout, and work around the clock, particularly if your pet is fast asleep on your lap.

A schedule can assist you in getting into the habit of engaging in healthful activities. You develop momentum to keep doing something once you've done it a few times. For example, going to the gym, hiking with your dog, attending a yoga class, or spending time in nature are all good ideas.

Even if you take a break from work and finish later, schedule time for these activities, keep yourself hydrated and regularly get up from your computer. If you can, adopt healthy eating habits. Remember to take care of your emotional health as well. Make sure to enjoy your victories and accomplishments rather than working yourself to exhaustion and burnout. If you feel the need to see a therapist, schedule an appointment. Do whatever it takes to ensure your health and happiness.

Physical Equipment Needed for Working from Home

I've been working remotely for the past five years and writing about it for nearly as long. I've worked from Airbnb's, coffee shops, co-working spaces, vehicles, and my own house, and one thing I've found is that the tools you use and how you set up your workspace have a significant impact on productivity and well-being. In addition, there are numerous low-cost options available to improve your environment, boost your productivity, and make you a happier and healthier remote worker.

Whether you're new to working from home or have been doing so for a long time, there are six essential items of equipment to consider.

- Noise Cancelling Headphones.
- Laptop Stand.
- Wireless Keyboard and Mouse.
- External Monitor.
- Office Chair.
- Standing Desk.

Noise Cancelling Headphones

Headphones are a must if you work with other people. They help block out distractions and reduce echo and feedback on workplace calls, allowing you to focus on the task at hand. Always go for active noise-canceling headphones, as they perform a better job of blocking out extraneous noise. This is beneficial at home and essential if you need to work from a crowded coffee shop or airport.

Laptop Stand

Repetitive strain injuries are a major danger for those who work from home. It's all too easy to find yourself positioned awkwardly on the sofa or at a table or workstation that's too low for extended computer use. Laptop supports exist in various designs, sizes, and prices, with several low-cost ones available. Ensure that it has adjustable height settings and is large enough to accommodate your laptop model.

Wireless Keyboard and Mouse

When you work from home regularly, it's critical to create an atmosphere that meets your requirements. Even if it's only for a short time, you should consider your home workstation to be a true office. To avoid spending more time charging than using your keyboard, look for one with long battery life. A mouse is the same way. If you're used to using one at work, you'll want one at home as well.

External Monitor

If you're used to working with a huge monitor or many displays, a laptop screen alone might not be enough. As a result, make sure to purchase one at a reasonable price to meet your requirements. If you have to pack up your home office every day or want to work and travel in the future, a portable monitor gives you greater freedom.

Office Chair

Office chairs are more expensive, but they make a significant difference. Given the amount of time you'll be sitting in it, your chair must be both comfortable and the right height for your desk. To meet your demands, look for one with lumbar support and height adjustability.

Standing Desk

If you're used to working from a standing desk or want to give it a try, you may do so without breaking the bank at home. For example, you may change your ordinary desk or kitchen counter into a standing one by placing a simple converter on top of it.

Remote Work from Psychological and Sociological Perspectives

Although scientific research has long emphasized the advantages of remote working, such as improved employee morale, health and well-being, and productivity, this was before the pandemic. The study assumed that working from home was a choice rather than a necessity and that companies offered both telecommuting and in-person options. Employees gravitated to the alternative that best matched their circumstances (e.g., commuting time, location, physical space, and the necessity for in-person meetings), as well as their personalities, as a result of this arrangement.

A study based on a psychological perspective stated that the effect of remote working on our brains is similar to the harm caused by the excessive use of social media. And this is among those unfavorable outcomes that suggest that we shouldn't do remote work for a longer period of time. Not least because of these shifts' rapid and nonvoluntary nature, there are troubling signals, or at least plausible grounds, to foresee unfavorable outcomes of long-term remote labor.

Loneliness

Isolation from others is a serious issue. Many employees feel lonely if employers do not invest in the necessary support networks and build virtual cooperation and a togetherness culture. Unfortunately, not every manager is prepared to make the switch from analog to digital management. Worse, the crisis may exacerbate existing inequities, further affecting women and minorities.

Anxiety

Anxiety is triggered by uncertainty. Most humans are prewired to optimize their habitats for boredom and predictability, despite all the talk about agility, adaptation, accepting uncertainty, and prospering in a VUCA (volatility, uncertainty, complexity, and ambiguity) environment. We can even force ourselves into believing that we have a higher level of certainty than we do. We crave significance; therefore, we feel insecure when we don't have it. When we are unable to plan, we feel uncomfortable and powerless. All of this means that remote working isn't nearly as difficult as the thought of doing it indefinitely. We have no idea what it implies for our overall life goals and lifestyle. We can't make critical logistical decisions like where to live, what to expect for our long-term professional prospects and employability, or how to manage our personal lives and relationships.

Stress

Any kind of change causes anxiety and stress. As a result, whether or not people have previously worked remotely is the single strongest predictor of how well they would cope with remote work. There is a significant difference between those who chose remote work before the crisis and continue to do so and those who were compelled to do so. You're in luck if your new normal looks a lot like your old one. The entire playing field is disrupted because most people do not fall into this category. Those that do are likely to have detrimental domino consequences on those who should not be affected. People who had always worked from home had to adjust to others who were compelled to transition to virtual work or cease working entirely. There's also a big difference in people's ability to move to remote employment, depending on whether or not they have kids.

There is no substitute for face-to-face conversation.

Fourth, replacing millions of years of in-person engagement with electronically mediated or virtual conversations is not viable. If zoom and other such tools have helped us duplicate some of the benefits of face-to-face communication, it's due as much to technology as it is to the power of human imagination. It's intriguing to consider that most of the technology we use and possibly even enjoy is designed to duplicate real-life experiences. However, most individuals believe that virtual interaction is only a cheap alternative for genuine contact and that beverages are preferable to Zinks. Perhaps the office's future duty will be to serve as a social theatre to get our daily dosage of face-to-face interaction.

Sociological perspective

Regardless of all the technological advances that have made it possible, teleworking is hardly a new concept. Working from home was the standard for craftsmen and peasants up to the 19th century, who conducted part or all of their employment in a place specifically aside for this purpose in their homes. Today, the coronavirus outbreak has reintroduced remote working into the mainstream, reigniting debate over its societal implications and impact on how we live. As teleworking became more popular as a cost-cutting tool, it also became more popular as a means of addressing other societal issues. For example, Teleworking was identified as a solution to address difficulties connected to work-life balance or low birth rates in a society with a larger participation of women in the labor market. All home members had to manage work with domestic tasks and childcare.

Work-life balance (under certain conditions)

One major benefit of teleworking is that it helps people better reconcile their professional and personal lives (often referred to as "work-life balance"). This is a topic of significant interest in countries where domestic and childcare responsibilities have shifted from solely the responsibility of one family member (typically the woman) to being a shared occupation by all household members. At the same time, they all work outside the home.

A few studies have looked into the link between teleworking and job satisfaction and found it favorable. However, the effect is not linear in this scenario, and the benefits tend to fade away as the intensity of teleworking increases. This is linked to the loss of social contacts and increased sensation of isolation that intensive teleworking can cause.

Balance with limitations

As is customary, the evidence to date addresses some of the concerns asked but leaves much more unresolved. How can it be, for example, that teleworking fails to show significant improvements in the age-old difficulty of achieving a work-life balance? Finally, teleworking saves us time commuting and allows us to integrate professional and domestic activities more easily.

Let me point out a few factors that limit the benefits of teleworking. For starters, just as teleworking makes it simpler to keep work from interfering with our personal lives, a term we'll abbreviate as WIF (work interferes with family), the literature also looks into the reverse effect: our personal lives interfering with our professional lives (FIW). It is believed that the greater the intensity of teleworking, the lower the WIF but the higher the FIW. It's simple to see how teleworking, for example, blurs the line between family and professional responsibilities. Thus, while teleworking allows people to swap jobs more easily, which might help them achieve a better work-life balance, it also increases the risk of FIW. In other words, it raises the risk of interruptions and other issues emerging from the domestic and family environment, which might impede job performance.

Second, the servitude induced by the digital link has been identified as a possible mitigating element in the relationship between teleworking and work-life balance. The technological interface that permits teleworking can also lead to longer working hours, for example, by forcing us to check our emails continuously, even outside of typical business hours. Teleworking would not be expected to improve work-life balance if it largely led to greater working hours.

Cultural Obstacles of Remote Work

Remote employment is becoming more common as a result of advancements in internet communication and collaboration capabilities. In the last 15 years, the number of Americans working from home has more than doubled.

Have No Fear, Remote Work Is Here!

Employees gain flexibility, avoid long commutes (which have a negative impact on job satisfaction), and are free of office distractions due to this approach.

On the other hand, remote work programs have one significant drawback: they frequently obstruct firms' efforts to develop and consolidate their corporate culture. For example, employees come together and participate in team-building events and division- or company-wide gatherings, which help to promote company culture. But, of course, it goes without saying that having dispersed teams can make this difficult.

Creating a corporate culture isn't simply a nice thing to do; it significantly impacts staff retention, satisfaction, and productivity.

The reason for this is simple: employees who identify with a company's values are more inclined to engage with their work, which is crucial in today's workplace. According to one study, businesses with high levels of engagement had higher levels of customer loyalty, productivity, and profitability than their competitors. Furthermore, businesses with high employee turnover rates frequently have low employee engagement.

Organizations with an engaged staff and a well-defined culture, on the other hand, are more likely to attract top talent. Leadership teams cannot underestimate the importance of defining corporate culture when investing in long-term success.

Work-from-home policies can have a range of effects on how a company's culture develops. For example, excessive telecommuting can have the following cultural effects:

1. Colleagues and teams are separated from one another.

Employees who work largely or solely from home are likely to communicate with their coworkers via email and phone calls. Working from home does not allow one to form meaningful relationships with coworkers in the same way working in an office.

This is significant for a few reasons. For starters, dealing with employees daily makes it easier to set expectations. When new employees are exposed to their coworkers' conduct regularly, they can comprehend the company's performance and communication standards far more rapidly than they would if they worked remotely. Second, workplace engagement and pleasure are highly linked to social connection. Those with a "best" work buddy are "seven times more likely to be engaged in their professions, are better at engaging customers, generate higher quality work, [and] have higher well-being," according to a Gallup survey of more than 15 million employees.

2. Remote employees' feelings of loneliness

Working from home may appear to make life easier at first, but it can harm employees' mental health. Humans are social beings, and working in an environment where no one sees them can make them feel alone.

Have No Fear, Remote Work Is Here!

Working from home can often be stressful. According to a recent study, a lack of intimate touch impairs the development of trust, connection, and common purpose, all of which are essential components of any successful working relationship. In addition, remote workers are more prone to suffer from workplace politics, fearing that their coworkers' gossip about them and campaign against them.

3. It's more difficult to cultivate enthusiasm for starting and growing a firm.

You want your staff to be enthusiastic about their work. It's not impossible, but it's certainly not easy to instill passion in a dispersed workforce. Also, it's difficult to generate passion for your service or product without a lot of social engagement unless your staff is 100% naturally motivated—high spirits are difficult to portray digitally.

4. Maintaining Employee Morale

Even in the best of times, employee morale is a major concern. It's even more important with a remote workforce because it's easy for engagement to decrease when people feel cut off from the wider picture.

Businesses can work on developing a good environment with robust internal communications to fight this difficulty. While the need for crucial information distribution is apparent in uncertain times, businesses must strike a balance between cold hard facts and softer, more human storytelling. To keep your crisis communications optimistic, look for instances of positive answers to problems throughout your internal community.

Leaders are required a prominent role to play in fostering a positive culture and gaining employee support. CEOs and important actors should utilize their clout to convey hope and togetherness, demonstrating to employees that their concerns are shared across the organization. Write blogs, be active on social media, and use video content and live broadcasts to keep your leadership apparent.

5. Creating Opportunities for Collaboration

Collaborative organizations are five times more likely to be high-performing than non-collaborative firms. Teams can no longer rely on being in the same area simultaneously to collaborate in a remote working environment, putting effective teamwork at risk. As a result, firms must employ digital tools to link individuals and overcome the physical obstacles that inhibit collaboration.

Collaboration allows remote workers to socialize with coworkers regardless of their location. Collaboration promotes a positive corporate culture and helps to retain the distinct subcultures that different departments thrive on. Dedicated workplaces for teams and extracurricular groups provide open platforms for networking, assisting remote workers in overcoming isolation and increasing communication.

6. Speak Your Employee's Language and Make Mobile Access Available

Some people may feel left out when working remotely, while others may feel overwhelmed by the drastic change in their working environment. When employees rely on technology to execute their jobs, ensuring proper tool access becomes vital.

Make information and communications available in the user's native language. For example, multilingual translation democratizes communication and gives employees a consistent experience regardless of where they work. Similarly, mobile digital workplace access allows users who do not have access to a computer to stay connected via their phones.

7. Time Zone Differences

Those awful time zones are related to being or feeling out of the loop. For example, you may wake up just as your teammate is going to bed. That means you can't always count on a teammate to answer a pressing query or assist you with a pressing need.

What is the solution? A four-hour time difference:

Working remotely, to be successful, usually necessitates some overlap with your coworkers' hours...we've discovered that a good four hours of overlap is required to prevent collaboration delays and feel like a team. If you're in Los Angeles and working with someone in New York, this isn't a problem; however, if you're in Chicago and working with someone in Copenhagen, it can be difficult. We couldn't avoid it; we had no choice but to compromise. We managed it by having Copenhagen work from 11 a.m. to 7 p.m. local time and Chicago work from 8 a.m. to 5 p.m. local time — just enough time for the crucial four hours of intersection.

When working with individuals in different time zones, remote employees must be adaptable. For example, you'll have to be more deliberate about when you send messages to others — and you'll have to stop checking your phone for notifications when you're not working. But there's another advantage: you may shift your workaround as needed, and you can delegate work to others who can finish it during their day and return it to you.

Weighing Up the Pros and Cons of Remote Working

Let's face it, no matter where you work, you're still doing the same thing: working. So, should you work from home or a place of business? It all boils down to the setting in which you'll be most effective, as well as the industry you're in. (Not to mention how lovely your home office is.) Remote working has been a part of the workforce in all industries for quite a while now. It's happened out of necessity at times, and it's happened out of choice at other times. However, the digital revolution, which began in the mid-late 1990s, ushered in a new era of remote employment. The most significant difference was that occupations that required a worker to sit at a desk and use a computer could theoretically be performed from home. With advancements in technology and lower internet and mobile phone expenses, this potential became an actual possibility, which many businesses have embraced. The ability to seek flexible working hours from your employer was codified in legislation in 2014. (With some conditions). Has the rising use of remote work had a beneficial or bad impact? Take a look at the benefits and drawbacks if you're thinking about it for yourself or your staff.

Pros of Remote Working:

The advantages of remote work can be separated into two categories: those that are primarily beneficial to the company and those that considerably improve the employees' quality of life. On the other hand, most of these items help both parties in the long run, as employee and employer pleasure are inextricably linked.

Employee Advantages

A more favorable work-life balance

Remote working gives you the freedom to choose your hours and, as a result, more opportunities to spend time with family and friends. In addition, it allows employees to create a timetable that best suits their preferences, rather than following the inflexible work plan imposed by the employer, which ignores any personal demands.

Employees may spend more quality time with their loved ones and take care of their personal needs when they need to be cared for by not spending time commuting and/or being at the office for a set length of time. This improves our work-life balance and, as a result, makes us happy.

Advantages to your health

When you work behind a desk, it can be difficult to maintain a good diet and lifestyle. How many office employees make sure we always have a nutritious, balanced meal to bring to work with us instead of grabbing whatever is available at the local restaurant or taking time to be physically active between work hours?

Remote working makes it much easier to keep a healthy diet (since you always have a fully equipped kitchen on hand), and it also gives you more time and flexibility to schedule workouts between work hours.

Employees who have a great work-life balance are less likely to be stressed and burn out, in addition to their physical well-being.

Obviously, not being in an office all of the time necessitates some effort to keep a reasonable work schedule and stay motivated (more on that later), but the ability to take a break whenever you need it trumps that.

There is no need to commute.

How many folks have you met who like their work commute? It's fine if the "commute" is a 15-minute walk to work, but going to work and back takes hours every day for many individuals.

What's worse, many employers don't count commute time as part of the hours worked, meaning it comes out of our personal time—time that could be better spent on family, friends, hobbies, and so on.

Working from home (or a local coffee shop/co-working space, whichever is more convenient) is better for the environment, the individual, and the organization.

Employer Advantages

The pool of talent has been greatly expanded

Consider how restricted your employment prospects are if you're only looking for people in your area (or have to relocate people there, which many people don't want to do). Your skill pool is literally the entire planet when you work remotely. So, is the ideal candidate for your team on the other side of the globe? It's no problem. Great individuals can do amazing things everywhere, as the saying goes. And you shouldn't have to miss out on all of these wonderful folks.

Engagement and loyalty

Working remotely builds trust, assuming the folks you employ are a good fit and everything works well (we'll go through the hiring process in detail later). Having faith in your team and what you're doing is what trust is all about. Likewise, increased loyalty is a result of confidence and personal engagement in what you're doing.

Productivity gains for employees

Employees that work remotely have greater freedom to work at their most productive periods. The "traditional" working hours are from 9 a.m. to 5 p.m. There are a few hypotheses about why, ranging from the British Industrial Revolution, which demanded optimal output on production lines, to make the most of the daylight before electricity.

Regardless of where this practice began, the main conclusion is that people and their unique requirements are anything but traditional.

We have morning, afternoon, and night people, as well as everyone in between. Employees who set their hours can figure out when they're most effective and work at those times. Working when people are most productive benefits both the employees (feeling productive makes us feel accomplished) and the employer—who wouldn't want their staff to be doing their best work, no matter what time it is?

Working with a remote team offers people the freedom to lean into their skills, which is one of the best things. Moreover, all kinds of inclinations and productivity tricks are accommodated in the remote culture.

Cost-cutting

Offices are costly. The cost of office equipment is high. Having a completely remote crew eliminates all of that. Providing your employees with the required equipment for working from home is wonderful, but it isn't equivalent to paying for large office space (or even numerous office spaces worldwide) plus commute costs.

You can have a headquarters if you want one, but it will be far smaller (and hence less expensive) than what you'd need if everyone on your team worked from there.

Buffer's Joel Gascoigne has a wonderful piece outlining all of the numerous options available to remote teams for their distribution pattern, including:

- Office-based with the option of working from home.

- A team that works remotely and is based in the same time zone.

- A global remote team that spans multiple time zones.

- A nomadic team with a fully scattered team.

Furthermore, as a remote team, you have the freedom to choose where your headquarters should be located, if necessary, which means that instead of San Francisco, London, or Berlin, you can choose a location that makes the most financial sense for your organization and budget.

The aspect of happiness, in my opinion, is the most important benefit. Trusting and empowering your staff to work responsibly and professionally while also giving them the freedom and flexibility to deal with all the large and small things that life throws at us results in great morale, pride, and loyalty.

Cons of Remote Working

Let's speak about the dark side of the moon now that we've demonstrated that working remotely provides numerous advantages for both the employee and the business. However, as appealing as remote work may appear, it is not without drawbacks, particularly when establishing a good team culture — one of the most significant hurdles that remote teams face.

Challenges, on the other hand, do not necessarily have to be negative. In a distributed workplace, extra effort is required in certain areas, particularly communication and transparency, to ensure that geographical distances — however large they may be — do not translate into communication gaps between team members.

Let's go over some of the most typical concerns that can arise when working from home.

Communication

While working in an office may appear to be the worse of the two options, there are some advantages (or should we say modest redeeming aspects), one of which is direct and immediately available human communication. All of your employees are in the same room, and within easy reach, so all you have to do is stroll over to them when you have a topic to discuss.

It's also a lot easier to comprehend face-to-face communication. Many publications and other resources teach you how to create rapport with people and get to know them to place a strong emphasis on things that can only be observed and done when you're in the same room as them. We catch up on people's facial expressions, body language, and general "feel" subconsciously in person and adapt our speech accordingly.

Because remote work eliminates the face-to-face aspect, communication becomes much more difficult. It's not impossible to overcome, but it's something to keep in mind and work on regularly. It depicts that communication in a remote team must be treated as a separate issue and addressed regularly.

In most remote teams, communication is the key to resolving this problem. The greatest method to solve a problem is to talk about it honestly. Avoid blaming others and try to find a solution. It's critical with remote teams even to overshare information. Mistaken assumptions, a lack of information, and insufficient communication are the root causes of many misunderstandings.

A Lack of Discipline

Working at an office can be motivating in and of itself, not to mention compel you to act motivated. People work, or at least make an effort to work, for a variety of reasons:

1. They can see that other people around them are working.

2. They would notice that they were slacking off because of the other individuals surrounding them.

There is no pressure to work in a friendly office environment when you work remotely. There is no one to remind or nudge you to do your work on time (efficiently). If you work from home the majority of the time, there are no people around to function as a motivational element in and of themselves—you must be that motivating force for yourself.

Keeping a tight schedule

There are numerous apps and solutions available to assist you in staying on top of your to-do lists. You name it: Todoist, Asana, Habitica, and so on. Such task apps ensure that you always have all you need in front of you and that you can quickly track your progress.

Keeping track of your (productive) hours

It's critical to know how much work you completed on any given day, especially if you don't have to work a conventional 9-5 schedule, to ensure you complete the required amount of work.

Tracking your time by task might also help you figure out what you spend the most time on during the day or week (and maybe see the things you should be spending even more or less time on). Toggle Track is an obvious choice for time management.

Work-life balance is important (the bad side of it)

When you start working from home instead of going to an office, the boundaries between work and personal life become a lot less clear — you're in a comfortable and familiar environment where you also do all of your day-to-day personal home stuff, which can potentially detract from the concentration you're supposed to put into your job.

Distractions

There are certainly some distractions in the office (especially if you work in an open office with no way to hide from what's going on around you), but it's a lot worse when you're on your own — especially if you're not used to set your schedule and don't have a lot of self-discipline, to begin with.

On the job, obnoxious and chatty coworkers can be annoying, but you have various things to worry about at home. Do you have children? While it's good to have more time with them, they may not realize that certain hours are reserved for work.

Technology Dependency

Technology is incredible. It's essentially the foundation that allows remote teams to interact effectively across vast geographical distances while also getting their work done. We've arrived at a position where internet tools like chat apps, time tracking, task boards, and online conference rooms allow for seamless communication and productive work even when team members are located on opposite sides of the globe.

However, technology, at least where we are now, does occasionally fail. Murphy's law dictates that it always happens at the worst possible time. Anyone who has ever worked remotely understands how frustrating it is to take 15 minutes to set up a video chat, have it fail every 10 minutes, and then wait for individuals to resolve their network access issues.

A technology failure in the office affects everyone at the same time. If you're on your own and a piece of technology that's crucial to your job breaks down, you're the weak link, and it could have a detrimental impact on everyone else's work.

There are ways to plan for this, and most remote teams have created their internal band-aids for dealing with technology failure, but it's something to keep in mind.

Have No Fear, Remote Work Is Here!

SPECIAL BONUS!

Want this book for FREE?

Get **FREE,** unlimited access to it and all of my new books by joining the Fan Base!

SCAN W/ YOUR CAMERA TO JOIN!

CHAPTER 2: REMOTE WORK IMPLEMENTATION

This chapter covers a step-by-step process to implement a remote work team; the project management tools help manage a team. It also includes tricks to ensure employee engagement, the challenges faced by the employees, and the solutions to cope with them.

How to set up a Remote Team as an Employer

Remote teams contribute to the company's profitability by lowering operating costs, increasing productivity, and lowering employee turnover. Setting up a successful remote team, on the other hand, takes time, effort, strategy, and execution.

Here are a few things required to start a remote team:

1. Determine the purpose.

Always determine the purpose before starting a new venture or undertaking a new activity. The objective clarifies your company's "why." Purpose gets things started and plots the road for where you want your company to go.

Before you construct your remote team, you must first define your purpose, as it will lead you through the entire preoperative stage. You'll know who to hire and what qualities to search for in potential employees. It will help you clarify your objectives and, more significantly, build the perfect productivity culture in your company.

2. Make the project manager or team leader a priority.

Once you've decided to form a remote team, the project manager is the first person you'll need to hire. The project manager, sometimes known as the team leader, is the person in command of the remote team.

In the remote team, he will be your eyes and ears. Everything passes through the project manager in the organizational hierarchy. You'll confer with him, and he'll report to you directly. His major role is to ensure that the remote team stays on track to meet the established goals.

3. Set up the frameworks

It's critical to establish frameworks when working with virtual teams, particularly with virtual assistants who come from remote regions where cultural, social, and time zone disparities are common.

Frameworks help to keep things running smoothly. The many areas of responsibility are identified, and the associated tasks are summarized for everyone's convenience. Create an organizational chart to show everyone where they fit into the company. This clears up any ambiguity and keeps team members from overstepping their bounds.

4. Define the workflows.

A workflow diagram depicts how workflows work through an operational funnel. Each responsibility area has its own workflow. A workflow's objective is to make work more efficient by specifying the procedure.

A workflow for an accounting project, for example, would look like this:

Client uploads files to CRM > Account Officer downloads file > Assigns to encoders > Head Auditor reviews work > Head Auditor transfers files to Account Officer > Account Officer uploads files and notifies client > Client downloads file from CRM.

5. Establish operational guidelines.

The only difference between operating a business in a physical location and in the virtual world is logistics. You must still ensure that the procedures that offer organization and efficiency in a brick-and-mortar firm are in place in the virtual world.

The Operational Guidelines are the standard reference guide. This includes not just the numerous workflows and framework definitions but also the organization's laws and regulations.

Your set of recommendations must answer all of the frequently asked questions. If a team member has any questions or concerns, the Guidelines should provide the answers.

Ensure everyone on the team has read it and then set up a half-day to go over its provisions.

6. Hire the best people for the job.

Choosing individuals for your remote staff might be a difficult task. There is a lot of talent throughout the planet. It's difficult to compare the achievements of one candidate to those of another because the circumstances are so varied.

This is why, rather than concentrating just on the candidate's resume and technical and fundamental skills, you should concentrate on his behavioral profile.

Know that your remote team may be made up of people from many nationalities, each with its own set of cultural and social norms. All members of the remote team must get along.

You can examine the candidate's behavioral profile in several ways:

- Create a set of three short essay questions that will require the candidate to go deeply into his own mind. Consider the following scenario: Your ship sank, and there was room in the lifeboat for one more passenger. Which do you think you'd rather save: your child or your mother?

- Inquire about the candidate's five non-negotiable fundamental values and why they were chosen.

- Give each candidate a job to complete with the group, and then assess their success based on how well they completed it.

It's critical to construct a team of people that can collaborate and respect each other's social and cultural differences. Within an organization, the conflict will always exist, but people who understand each other will seek to resolve it quickly.

7. Create a technological profile.

You should now construct the technological profile after you've put up the foundations and operations. The technological profile is a list of the programs and gear you'll need to run your business. It's commonly broken down into the following sections:

- Collaboration.
- Sharing of files.
- File Protection.
- Communication.
- Maintenance/Repair.

The programs must be installed on everyone's PCs on the team. To avoid work halting and further delays, all gear must be in good functioning order.

8. Create an evaluation procedure.

The only way to assess the team's performance is to conduct regular evaluations.

Create a performance formula to assess the quality of each team member's work. If you're operating a lead-generating campaign, for example, a sample evaluation process might be:

- 50 percent accuracy; ability to obtain reliable information.
- Statistics show that 40% of all contacts are related.
- Work ethics; attitude, general behavior, and punctuality = 10%.

Compile the data weekly and distribute a copy of the month-end evaluation to your team members. This will be the criterion for judging their performance in the coming month.

9. Arrange for weekly meetings.

One of the most important qualities to have in a company is communication. Effective communication channels lessen the likelihood of casual mistakes, oversights, and misunderstandings.

This is the benefit of having weekly meetings arranged. You'll be able to keep the team up to date on new developments and handle any pending issues or concerns. End-of-week meetings are crucial for laying the groundwork for the next week.

It's also an opportunity for you to strengthen your bonds with your coworkers. This enhances communication channels and encourages trust, transparency, and respect.

Setting up a remote team comes with its own set of obstacles. However, as long as you create the ground rules and criteria for assembling the team you want, you will be able to put together a group of people with whom you can grow your firm.

Necessary Digital Tools for Remote Working

Although remote work is becoming more popular, 41% of employees are employed by organizations that do not provide work-approved mobile communication solutions. It isn't only inefficient but also exposes your firm to security threats by relying on non-work-approved BYOD devices.

We believe it is critical to identify and deploy the latest remote technologies that will keep your team connected, organized, and safe in the age of the anyplace office. Here are the five technologies changing the way people work remotely and why your hybrid business should think about incorporating them into your procedures.

Remote Teams: What Tech Tools Do They Need?

Businesses should prepare for this development by deploying the correct tech stack as more employees desire to work remotely. Your remote workers will require tools for:

Business Management: Accounting, documentation, human resources, and other corporate necessities.

Communication: Quick check-ins, meetings, feedback, conferences, and webinars.

Project Management: Task tracking, time management, prioritization, delegation, and cooperation.

Data and security: Safeguarding communication over public internet routes while protecting and storing sensitive information.

Freelance Marketplaces: Find and hire remote workers with built-in scalability and flexibility.

There are several tools available that deal with the business's behind-the-scenes cleaning so you can focus on what you do best.

Remote Work Tools for Human Resources and Payroll

1. Workful

Workful is a simple and affordable HR and payroll management solution for small businesses. The simple dashboard can be used to file tax returns, sync timesheets, and keep track of your employees' information, time management, and paid time off.

2. Zenefits

Onboarding, benefits, payroll, and paid time off are all rolled into one simple platform with Zenefits. Zenefits offers a 14-day free trial for entrepreneurs and small and midsize businesses (roughly 25 to 1,000 employees).

3. Rippling

Rippling, like Zenefits, is an all-in-one employee management platform for your HR and IT requirements. With various pricing models to suit your needs, you can manage your employees' payroll, benefits, devices, and apps.

4. Namely

Namely is a people management platform for small and midsize businesses that boost employee engagement and productivity. On a cloud-based, user-friendly platform, Namely manages HR, payroll, benefits, and talent management. Its six-to-eight-week deployment procedure, supervised by Namely experts, makes switching HR systems simple.

5. Gusto

Gusto is a small business people platform. The app allows you to run payroll, manage benefits, onboard your team, use time-tracking and time-off-request tools, handle state and federal taxes, and consult with HR experts all in one place.

6. QuickBooks

QuickBooks by Intuit includes all of the accounting software you'll need to keep track of your sales and costs, generate profit and loss reports, pay employees and vendors, and track delinquent invoices. For quick consolidation, QuickBooks can connect to business bank accounts as well as PayPal and Square.

7. Wave

Wave is an accounting software platform that allows you to track your income and spending, create invoices, take payments, pay personnel, and scan receipts. It is intended for entrepreneurs, small enterprises, independent contractors, and sole proprietors.

Remote Work Tools for Cloud Computing

Cloud computing allows IT resources to be delivered on-demand. Cloud computing is cost-effective, scalable, and easy since it eliminates the need for physical equipment and in-house infrastructure. The big three public cloud providers are listed below. Keep in mind that cloud brokers can help you mix and match cloud services to best suit your needs.

8. Amazon Web Services (AWS)

Amazon Web Services (AWS) is a highly customizable cloud-based software that provides integrated web services to businesses and people. It was created in 2006. AWS is a dominant name in creative cloud computing, with three pricing plans and a 12-month free tier. AWS is the industry leader, offering over 175 services.

9. Microsoft Azure

Microsoft Azure, which was released in 2010, is a Windows and Linux-compatible solution with a "cloud-first" approach that is ideal for any business. Microsoft Azure offers a free 12-month trial and a cost calculator to help you figure out how much its various products and services cost.

10. Google Cloud Platform

Google Cloud is a user-friendly cloud services provider with powerful machine learning and artificial intelligence (AI) capabilities. Google is known for its open-source technologies and innovative culture. New clients can get a free three-month trial and $300 in credits to try out Google Cloud's goods and services.

Tools for Team Collaboration

Finding the best communication software for your remote staff is critical to your company's success. Adopt products that help teams collaborate, organize, and communicate more effectively.

11. Slack

This is company-wide collaboration software that aims to replace internal email. Slack, the most popular and expensive service of its sort, offers channels as organizing places to collaborate on various projects or themes. Slack may have various functionality deficiencies that might prompt you to explore elsewhere, such as limiting the searchable chat history, depending on your sector.

12. Chanty

Chanty is an AI-powered online chat platform for small and medium-sized businesses. Unlike Slack, Chanty does not limit the amount of message history that may be searched. Chanty organizes all files, projects, and chats into folders using Teambook, an organizational feature.

13. Microsoft Teams

Teams are appropriate for firms currently using Microsoft products because it is tightly linked with other Microsoft Office tools. You can use real-time access, sharing, and editing of documents and host audio, video, and web conferences. The Teams UI is more ordered and segmented than Slack and Chanty, which may prevent open communication.

Tools for Videoconferencing and Remote Work

14. GoToMeeting

LogMeIn's GoToMeeting is a mobile-friendly, stand-alone web conferencing and video conference software that's ideal for online meetings. Monthly payment choices range from $14 to $19. The Professional plan can accommodate up to 150 people, while the Business plan can handle up to 250 people. Screen sharing, recording, and transcription are all available through GoToMeeting and GoToWebinar, and GoToTraining solutions for large-scale virtual events with up to 3,000 participants.

15. Zoom

Zoom is a basic video conferencing and video chat service that offers free and premium subscriptions ($14.99 to $19.99 per month for Zoom Pro and Zoom Business plans, and $30 per month for Zoom United Pro). With the large meeting add-on, the platform can hold up to 1,000 attendees and 49 movies on a single screen, making it ideal for huge audiences. Unlike some other platforms, which limit the number of simultaneous video feeds, anybody in a Zoom conference can have a high-definition video feed and the camera turned on. File sharing, a searchable history, and a 10-year archive are all available with the team chat function.

16. BlueJeans

This California-based firm, which was founded in 2009, provides interoperable, cloud-based videoconferencing with Dolby voice compatibility. It boosts productivity by integrating with over 30 apps and providing meeting highlights and transcription services. BlueJeans offers three pricing categories as well as a free seven-day trial.

Tools for Project Management

Your remote team can use project management and task management software to keep track of deadlines, resources, and deliverables.

Look for a project management software that has three major features to keep your team on track:

- Features allow your team to collaborate, share input, and ultimately complete tasks and projects more quickly.

- Time-tracking software can help you figure out how long projects take, how profitable they are, and how to get to project milestones faster in the future.

- Encourage team members to brainstorm and visualize ideas using visual collaboration tools.

17. Trello

With this simple method, you can see all of your company's projects at a glance. Trello is a graphically designed collaborative platform that organizes and prioritizes projects using Kanban boards, lists, and cards. Butler, a built-in workflow automation software, boosts productivity by automating tasks and finding inefficiencies on your behalf.

18. Click Up

ClickUp, which bills itself as "one app to replace them all," makes it simple to import content from other productivity and project management apps. From agile project management for company-wide efficiency to simple to-do lists, their software can handle everything. ClickUp is fully adjustable task management for any team, including a list, Kanban board, calendar view, and dependencies for each work. Some users, however, may find the inability to create user groups and subfolders to be a drawback.

19. Wrike

Wrike is an excellent project management application for mid-sized businesses with interactive Gantt charts, calendars, and drag-and-drop dashboards. Wrike is appealing because of its intuitive layout and support for repeating activities. Yet, the expensive price tag and absence of integrated live chat and invoicing leaves more to be desired. Wrike also has a smartphone application.

20. Miro

Miro is a simple collaborative whiteboarding software designed to boost dispersed team productivity. It's great for stimulating creativity and idea production. Consider a single large whiteboard that will never need to be erased. The interactive Miro Mind Map allows groups to collect and organize ideas instantly. It's a fantastic tool for designers, as it allows groups to collaborate on designs and discuss them in real-time.

How to Ensure the Engagement of Employees

By engaging remote employees, you can ensure that your team is as efficient and productive as if they were in the office. However, defining and measuring what employee engagement means to your team members can be tough.

Working remotely is difficult for many people since they are surrounded by distractions such as chores, housemates or roommates, social media, and television at home. Simply asking your employees about their work and their enthusiasm levels is the simplest approach to measure their levels of engagement. You can also keep track of their assignment progress and address any concerns you have about their performance.

Ways to keep remote workers engaged

Here are some ideas for keeping your company's culture alive while also making your virtual employees feel like they're part of the team.

1. Promote health and well-being.

The wellness of your employees should be your top priority. After all, if your staff are sick, they won't be able to perform at their best - or even at all. You might be able to incentivize your staff to go outside, cook a great meal, exercise, or develop a healthy habit. You could even launch a team-wide wellness program (30 days of yoga, one month of daily walks, etc.).

This will benefit your employees' health and bring them closer together and demonstrate your concern for their general well-being. Look for methods to make healthy behaviors more accessible, such as offering a longer lunch break for workouts or allowing them to leave early on a sunny day to enjoy the sunshine.

2. Host virtual meetings and informal get-togethers.

Many distant teams use video calls, instant messaging, email, and web conferencing systems to keep in touch regularly. A voice or video conferencing call can go a long way toward encouraging group cooperation while the entire team is working.

It's also crucial to schedule non-work-related virtual get-togethers. There's always something stressful to talk about at work, but you don't want every discussion to be uncomfortable and feared. To keep employees motivated and thrilled to be a part of the team, schedule work outings or casual video conversations.

3. Ascertain that employees are heard and respected.

Even from afar, your staff deserve to be valued. You should find simple ways to honor your employees as often as possible because you aren't in the office with them every day to say thank you or take them out to lunch for their work anniversary.

Is someone's birthday approaching? Send a virtual gift card to them. Has a coworker gone above and above on a project? Make a team call to thank them for their efforts. Look for small gestures that demonstrate you care about your employees.

4. Develop personal relationships.

While you want to maintain a professional demeanor with your employees, keep in mind that they are still people. They, like everyone else, have loved ones, celebrations, and terrible days. To better interact with your employees, you must understand their talents, weaknesses, and hobbies as an employer.

If remote employees realize you care about them as people and employees, they will be more engaged and dedicated to the firm and their roles.

5. Maintain open lines of communication.

Employees that work irregular hours or outside of the headquarters' time zone may believe that their team isn't available when they are, and vice versa.

While it's unreasonable to expect everyone to be present 24 hours a day, knowing that virtual workers can communicate with their coworkers and stay in touch via digital communication makes them feel more connected.

6. Make your teamwork more fun.

Gamification, or the application of game-playing features to non-game contexts, has become a popular strategy for businesses looking to increase consumer loyalty and engagement in a fun way. Employee engagement strategies that encourage competitions and awards for ordinary activities can be useful.

Ways to Make Sure That Your Remote Workers Are Working

You would think that some of the most important things to ask when it comes to monitoring employees who work from home are straightforward:

- Is my remote team operating during regular business hours?
- Is this a case of procrastination?
- How can I keep my remote staff productive?
- How can I keep track of my remote team's output?

Transparency, empathy, and collaboration, based on my own experience, are critical for increasing remote employees' creativity and productivity. So, I'll go over a few steps that I believe may be beneficial in this area.

1. Create a list of tasks with deadlines

This is a solution without a doubt. But I recommend that you go a step farther. Consider your work in terms of structure and procedures rather than a list of tasks. A task is essentially a core structural unit of your work, and in ActiveCollab, you can quickly assign tasks with deadlines. However, suppose your team does not completely comprehend the scope of their actions. In that case, every monitoring activity will be focused on a single outcome rather than leading your entire team to work together toward a common goal. As a result, the goal is to have a decent organization; assignments with deadlines are only a means to get there.

2. Observe team activity regularly

Transparency is essential when it comes to remote employment. Transparent workflows and objectives are only the beginning. It's time to involve your team and present them with a wider vision once you've planned and arranged everything on your end.

That way, each member of your team will understand where they fit in, what is expected of them, and what their deliverables are. In terms of inclusivity, each team member will understand how their contributions contribute to the overall goal, transforming each individual work into a team effort. Unless, of course, your team is a group?

It's a given that you'll communicate your expectations to the team and request their feedback, but involving everyone in the review process can elevate your team's work to a whole new level. If you really want your team to work as a unit, we recommend that you conduct regular checks on team activity and engage your entire team in those checks.

3. Keep track of how much time employees spend on the internet

No. Certainly not. I'm not going to urge you to intrude into your team's personal space, especially because we're seeing hundreds upon thousands of teams go entirely remote, in most cases working from their own homes. That is not the way to proceed.

Is there another option? It's all about transparency. Include your staff in every step of the planning process, be available to answer their questions, provide direction, and ensure that they know they have your trust. It's quite easy to stay ahead of any procrastination or slacking off without going too far when every step of the process and each assignment is put out in front of you.

4. Keep track of when employees are at their desks

Rather than tracking your staff, I recommend creating a set of rules and processes that will allow your team to arrange their time better so that they are not restricted to factory hours. If everything else fails, monitoring if your remote staff is sitting at their desktops, is a last resort. There's no reason why it should have to come to that.

If and when your team members begin to fall short of their daily goals, it's time to consider implementing a more rigid work schedule. Before you travel, you should speak with your team, learn about their problems, and have a deeper understanding of why they aren't achieving their objectives. There are certainly more compassionate ways to achieve monitoring objectives.

5. Supervise Employees Remotely

Transparency is, once again, the best form of oversight. But not the kind of transparency that necessitates the thirty-second screenshot of your employee's screen. Or, God forbid, putting in some other kind of intrusive tracking device.

Define a procedure that allows each member of your team to validate and provide feedback on each task. A shared effort that results in a common goal is one of the key pillars of every team. There's no reason not to include everyone in the validation step after including them in the planning and tracking phases.

This is more beneficial when your team is multidisciplinary, and members may contribute significantly to feedback and analysis of other people's work. Even if they can't, it's a great way to recognize each team member and shine a light on them. It's easier to spot problems, and it's a lot more enjoyable when the outcomes are generally acknowledged.

6. Summary of the Day's Report

Your team may lose sight of what they completed during the day if they are engaged in many projects simultaneously. However, your daily summary should not solely consist of a list of tasks completed. It can also be a tool for identifying areas for growth, laying out any possible problems, and outlining the activities your team has to take to achieve or overcome them.

You have full control over the format of these daily reports, but a regular team meeting is a great method to make sure that everyone is on track, that each task is validated, and that there are no misunderstandings.

Pillars to Build a Positive Workplace Culture

Seven pillars contribute to building a positive culture in workplaces, even for those working remotely. They are:

1. Transparency

Transparent businesses promote a free flow of communication and information throughout the organization, ranging from simple employee feedback to sharing profit-and-loss statements.

2. Positivity

Much is made of problem-solving, but positive, fresh approaches to confronting harsh truths, problems, and expected results focus on the company's strengths rather than its flaws.

3. Measurement

There is no better approach to assessing business success than collecting, measuring, and analyzing data.

4. Acknowledgment

The cultural chain's visible links that bind a workforce together are how a firm recognizes and rewards great work.

5. Uniqueness

The unique elements of a company's brand must be communicated and used across all product and service selling points. Google, for example, is known for its ground-up innovation, while Southwest Airlines is regarded for offering a more relaxed air travel experience than its competitors.

6. Listening

Listening is considered an active talent in effective business dealings. Many businesses rise above the competition by cultivating a culture that encourages active, results-oriented listening.

7. Mistakes

The stronger indicator of outstanding culture is how firms deal with failure rather than success. Is there anything they can take away from it? Can they take advantage of it and move forward?

Addressing Remote Working Challenges as an Employee

When working from home, it's critical to look after your mental health. Burnout is a serious medical issue that may easily affect those who work from home, although few people know it. In fact, 82 percent of remote workers stated they suffered from burnout while working from home, 52 percent said they worked more hours than they did in the office, and another 40% said they felt compelled to perform better and contribute more.

This demonstrates that working from home has genuine effects, especially if you are unprepared. If this is the first time you're working from home, it's critical to seek guidance from other remote workers to manage your mental health properly. Here are some helpful hints for young professionals working from home who want to take better care of their mental health.

Maintain a routine.

The distinctions between work and personal time can become blurred without consistent routines, which can be challenging to achieve. If you can, stick to your regular sleeping and working schedule. Wake up at the same hour every day, eat breakfast, and remove your jammies. Before checking in, schedule some "commute time" and spend it exercising, reading, or listening to music. Above all, when your workday is done, stop working. Turn off your computer, stop reading your emails, and concentrate on your personal life.

Create a pleasant working atmosphere.

Find a quiet place away from people and distractions like the TV if you can (or the kitchen, when you feel snacky). Before you start working, gather everything you'll need in one spot — chargers, pens, paper, and anything else - and close the door if you can. Even if you're working in a small or shared place, strive to set aside a space for work. Finally, choose a comfortable position.

Make sure you take regular breaks.

Working from home can make us feel obligated to be accessible at all times. However, being "present" is useless if your mental health is deteriorating. Making time for breaks is vital for managing stress — aim to take lunch and screen breaks regularly. Allow yourself time to focus on something else so that when you return, you will be more focused. Even 5 to 10 minutes of brief breaks every hour can help you be more productive.

Remember to communicate and interact.

Remote working has its perks, but it can also make you feel more alone. However, there are numerous methods to stay in touch with those who matter while also improving our mental health. Human interaction is important at business and at home, so schedule video calls and call instead of emailing. If you're having trouble working from home, talk to your coworkers or boss about your issues. Remember that your coworkers are probably in the same boat as you. Inquire about their well-being and see if there are any ways you can help each other. Schedule a digital coffee break or a Friday online get-together to connect electronically.

Recognize your limitations.

Setting boundaries with other household members is crucial to maintaining your mental health while working from home. Working remotely allows you to be more flexible, so take advantage of it. However, it can be tough if you have other distractions, such as children at home who may believe you are on vacation and want to spend time with you. Have a conversation with your family about your requirements. Explain to them that you still have work to accomplish and that you'll need some quiet time to complete it, and share your timetable with them. Set work boundaries in the same way. It's easier to stay logged on when your house serves as your office, but try to turn off your computer when the workday is done so you can spend time with your family.

Be kind to yourself.

Remember that this is a unique scenario, and everything will feel out of the ordinary. Be gentle with yourself and accept that you may not be as productive as you normally are. Be realistic and thoughtful about what you can achieve given the conditions, and unwind once you've completed your work.

Traits of Leaders Who Successfully Manage Remote Employees

While many of the characteristics that make a good manager differ depending on the organization, team, and manager, I have discovered a set of six personality qualities that are always present in the most effective remote team leaders based on my experiences. Some of these attributes may come naturally to you, while others will require effort on your part.

Indefatigable

You're on the right track if the prospect of attending a midnight meeting or holding a coaching session at 3 a.m. gives you a mental rush and a burst of energy. Managing remote teams frequently entails working across time zones and may necessitate working long days and strange hours. If you have a 9-to-5 attitude or find that your energy levels drop after a "regular day," trying to keep a constant stream of energy and enthusiasm may seem like a surefire way to burn out. To maintain performance steadily over lengthy periods, try adapting to a more flexible schedule by integrating pauses between work "sprints."

Company Evangelist

Remote workers require positive tales about brand messaging, corporate culture, and organizational principles, but feel-good marketing does not always translate effectively over phone lines, videoconferencing, and email. Communication becomes even more difficult when nasty, gossipy reports about who did what to whom to compete against. Remote team leaders who are extra optimistic, extra pro values, extra pro-culture, and extra pro-brand are the finest. If successful evangelism is to spread across the miles, it must be sincere. If your feelings about the company are simply lukewarm, consider sharing company success stories that demonstrate a genuine affection for the company, what it does, and the people it serves.

Encouraging

Remote employees, like everyone else, face roadblocks, and they require a strong leader who can keep them focused on solutions while communicating straightforwardly and positively. The most successful supervisors use optimism and good energy to motivate remote personnel. Set a positive example by approaching obstacles as exciting new opportunities to create something creative, engaging, and innovative. Pep talks don't have to be sophisticated to be effective. Just let folks know, "We struck a snag, but it's all right." This is something we can conquer. We'll figure it out together. We're going to pull it off."

Approachable

Open lines of communication help managers stay informed, but it's not always easy when staff is spread across the country rather than across the hall. Take it as a hint that you're not easily approachable if you're generally the last to hear bad news.

Approachability does not imply that you must be everyone's best buddy; rather, your staff must feel comfortable informing you of any news, good or bad. To make it safe for employees to discuss, you don't need to institute a full-time open-door policy, but you should establish clear standards for how and when you want to be contacted and express them to your team. The finest leaders talk to their remote personnel regularly and in a genuine way.

Constructive

Positive reinforcement is a favorite teaching method of all excellent leaders since it provides precise feedback such as, "That thing you just accomplished right now was really good." This motivates staff to keep up the excellent work you want to see.

When it comes to positive reinforcement, there are four main aspects to consider. First and foremost, make it meaningful so that there is a genuine learning curve. Second, provide them a clear image of the exact performance that is being praised for replicating it. Third, catch the personnel responsible for misbehaving. Positive reinforcement relies on a brain connection that links the reward to the desired behavior, and it must be supplied in real-time to be effective. Finally, don't let criticism taint the positive message. Constructive criticism has its place and time, but not while you're giving a positive message.

Leadership 2.0

One of the most challenging tasks of managing remote teams is dealing with the psychological distance that distant employees experience, influencing collaboration. Combating communication barriers helps to close the psychological gap. While email is generally the most popular method of communication among remote teams, it is also the most restrictive, and it poses the highest danger of message misinterpretation. The finest managers make remote connections feel more like face-to-face by frequently picking up the phone or video conferencing. They also encourage frequent, two-way communication, in which employees are encouraged to share their ideas, insights, and opinions.

How to Hire a Remote Team

Because not everyone is made out for remote work, you'll want to think about the talents required to succeed in this setting before hiring for a remote role.

Characteristics of a high-performing remote worker

There are a few characteristics that make great remote employees successful:

Proclivity for action: This type of individual will find something important to perform even if they aren't given a task list.

Ability to prioritize: When working remotely, it's common for critical duties to be unclear (especially at a startup). A person who can focus on the correct duties while ignoring the less important ones will succeed.

Writing skills: In a remote team, the majority of communication takes place via text—email, team chat, or one-on-one private communications. In a remote team, someone who struggles to write simply and concisely may struggle. It's also crucial to be able to communicate tactfully in writing. It's all too easy to come across as abrupt when communicating by text. Emojis, when used liberally, can go a long way.

Trustworthy: If you can't trust someone, not seeing them every day will cause you sleepless nights. Make certain that anybody you hire is someone you can trust.

Local support system: If a person's only support system is their workplace, working in a distant location is unlikely to be beneficial. You'll need folks with outside support networks who can communicate with others on a daily/weekly basis.

How to find remote candidates

Of course, it's hard to hire if you don't have any prospects for the job, so the first thing to think about is how people will learn about the opening. This is the area where we've had the most success.

Our networks: People you've already worked with are excellent prospects to join your team. This is especially true if you had a good time working with them and would like to do so again. Also, see if any of your clients, partners, investors, family, friends or anybody else you believe would be useful knows of any good prospects. People who aren't actively looking for work will often confide in a friend looking for work.

Local meetup groups: It may seem strange to propose local recruiting for a remote team, but it has shown to be beneficial in the past.

Your user base: If you're lucky enough to have a huge user base that meets the qualifications you're looking for; it might be a wonderful place to look for candidates. This can be accomplished by including a "hey, we're recruiting!" link in emails to the blog as well as on our website. When you have available positions, this results in dozens of daily applications. Furthermore, because they are already familiar with your firm and how you operate, your consumers are likely a good cultural fit.

Posts on your company's blog: You should write about how you work and your organization's culture. People that like how you work will be interested in finding out how they can collaborate with you.

Request assistance with sourcing from coworkers: Some firms take a highly aggressive approach to sourcing, mining every employee's social networks for potential job prospects. This hasn't been essential for me. Instead, simply ask your teammates to help you spread the news to gain a fantastic new teammate. People are often eager to work with and assist in selecting their new teammates, so involving them in the process benefits everyone.

Job boards: Job boards might be a good place to look for candidates. Just be wary of individuals seeking remote employment in general—anything that allows them to work from home—rather than your specific job. However, gold can be found here on occasion.

Share as much as you can: To let people know you're hiring, use Twitter, LinkedIn, Facebook, AngelList, and any other platform you have access to.

The wider your reach, the more likely your job posting will get up on the right person's desk.

Recruiting people for remote teams is often more difficult than you might anticipate. It can be challenging to get the word out about your firm and your positions because you don't have worldwide connections, you're a tiny brand, and local ties can be difficult to come by. Use every available channel to spread the news and keep track of where the best prospects come from.

Hiring process of a remote worker

If you've keenly followed the steps mentioned above, you must start receiving applications soon. It's time to make the hire, and this is when the real challenge begins. To locate the individual, you want, you'll have to sift through dozens, hundreds, or even thousands of applicants. Hiring takes time, but it's one of the most critical things you can do to ensure your team's success.

1. Establish a value-added application procedure.

Also, rather than asking for resumes, ask people to apply uniquely in the job posting. Instead, create a value-added application process that informs candidates about the position and informs the interviewing team about the individual. Instead of requesting a cover letter right now, have them compose a sample pitch email to a partner. People enthusiastic about your firm are more than eager to take on these extra responsibilities, and they often do so with pleasure. Those who aren't a good fit simply skip or forget to apply, turning the one-of-a-kind application process into a filter.

2. Make use of hiring technologies to aid in the creation of a unified recruiting experience.

I recommend using the TalentWall hiring management solution because it allows you to hire collaboratively, retain transparency throughout the search process, and guarantee that candidates receive timely check-ins. A recruiter may also examine how long it's been since they last spoke with a candidate using TalentWall.

Because communication in a remote team is frequently asynchronous, it's critical to provide a central location where everyone can readily get on the same page about the health and state of a recruitment process. Hiring managers can readily observe which candidates are progressing through the interview process with a platform like TalentWall. Recruiting and hiring managers may use the technology's data to identify changes to improve the whole interview process. Talentwall also keeps track of what's going on with applicant pipelines, both now and in the future. This allows hiring teams to spend more time focusing on challenges and strategy rather than rehashing the past.

You should also employ an applicant management system (ATS). I recommend that we adopt Greenhouse as our applicant tracking system, which allows us to construct intentional hiring plans that include:

-Interview stages: Before starting a search, try to define the interview procedure. This method aids in determining what candidates should expect throughout their interview with you.

-Interview questions: Make a list of interview questions that will assist your interviewers in determining whether candidates are qualified for a position.

-Interview scorecards: Determine how to assess if a candidate effectively interviews at each level of the interview process.

Creating a thorough interview plan, transparency for recruiting teams, and maintaining regular communication with candidates has led to meaningful interactions, a reduction in bias due to consistent evaluation, and keeps a search going ahead, in my experience.

3. Set up a video conference interview with the best candidates.

Candidates for the following phase, a recruiter interview, are chosen by the recruiter, recruiting manager, and other teammates who analyze applications. If the candidates pass the initial interview, they will be invited to the job fit interview. During the job fit interview, try to learn more about the individual and ask questions to see if they would be successful in a remote setting. Because these are best completed synchronously, make the most of your time by scheduling them back-to-back. This also allows you to compare prospects more readily. During this

Have No Fear, Remote Work Is Here!

stage of the process, pay close attention to how well the applicant communicates. In a distant position, effective communication is so important that even minor details might indicate whether or not someone is a good fit. Individuals that are bad at following up through email, forget when the interview was planned, or aren't flexible with an interview time in terms of time zones are all potential red flags.

4. Use a project to put top candidates to the test.

Following these video call interviews; a few prospects are likely to stand out as the best candidates. Put them to the test at this point by constructing a moderately tough task and representing the types of activities they'll accomplish daily, depending on the function. The job will almost always require the candidate to interact with team members – possibly more than once. You'll have an idea of how they interact and communicate this way. It should just take a few hours to complete the test.

5. Verify references before making an offer.

Use Skill Survey to send out an anonymous survey for a reference check before making an offer. This makes it easier to acquire open input from candidates' references.

Questions to Ask from A Remote Interviewer

You can use behavioral interviewing to see if individuals you're evaluating have the requisite attributes to succeed in a remote work setting. Behavioral interviewing helps to identify how people have acted in previous scenarios. Here are some possible questions to ponder.

Propensity towards action

- Tell me about when you took the initiative to introduce a new or alternative way of working at your organization.

- Tell me about a situation when you had limited information and had to make a decision.

Ability to prioritize

- Describe an occasion when you successfully delegated work.

- Tell me about a period when you had a lot of things on your mind. What exactly did you do?

Proficient writing

- Describe a concrete example of how you keep stakeholders informed about the development of your project.

- Describe an instance when you were speaking with someone via written communication, and they didn't understand what you were saying. What exactly did you do?

Trustworthiness

- Give a specific example of how you keep your boss up to date on what's going on in your department.

- Tell me about a time when you were honest despite the possibility of a negative outcome.

Tips for Optimizing Workflow of Remote Teams

It's common for remote workers to feel alienated, left out, and isolated when there's no face-to-face connection, leading to process breakdowns. A project's timeliness could be jeopardized in a matter of days. However, there are a few tactics that I've found to be effective in keeping work moving, even among teams that may never see each other.

1. Establish an assignment protocol

To ensure that nothing gets lost, remote work necessitates a systematic approach to work requests and assignments. Even in the closest office environment, informal, "drive-by," and verbal requests can be a problem, but when there are remote teams, the problem can quickly increase, and team leaders will have no idea who is working on what.

Establish a procedure for handling incoming work requests and dividing up responsibilities. It might be as simple as requiring all work requests to be directed to a specified email address.

Create request templates or brief creative templates to help team members understand expectations and have everything they require to get started once the assignment arrives.

2. Make use of document and asset storage

For remote teams, managing digital assets and ensuring that essential documentation is immediately available is a must. It's inconvenient and time-consuming to expect workers to email back and forth to request the information and assets they require, and it increases the chance of versioning problems.

Instead, use digital asset management (DAM) software, or even something as simple as Google Drive, Box, or Dropbox, to build a central store of documents and resource materials easily accessible. This eliminates the need for anyone to wait for items to arrive, allowing work to continue.

3. Make use of collaboration software

If proactive actions are not made to ensure inclusion, remote employees may feel isolated. In fact, nearly two-thirds of remote workers are concerned that their coworkers would modify project plans without informing them.

Use real-time collaboration technologies that capture the whole dialogue surrounding projects, plans, and progress — and show it in full view of the entire team — to avoid feelings of exclusion and help keep everyone in the loop.

For project-related communication, tools like Slack are far more transparent than email, and they ensure that vital input and feedback don't get lost in the email inbox dumpster fire.

4. Break Tasks Down into Subtasks

Although remote workers are more productive, it might not be easy to keep track of their complete work. It's easier to remain on top of project status for in-house teams, and it just feels safer when you see each other every day.

Transferring duties to distant workers, on the other hand, feels risky. Are they carrying out their responsibilities? Or are they ignoring the situation?

You may get a more granular and realistic perspective of project status, deadlines, and estimated completion durations using a system that tracks each work and allows you to divide larger tasks down into smaller subtasks.

It can also assist you in identifying bottlenecks along the road and resolving issues before a big snag catches the team off guard as the project nears completion.

5. Make live check-ins a priority.

The most effective teams, according to data, are those in which supervisors check in with remote workers frequently. Maintaining involvement, rapport, and, well, a team-like atmosphere requires a concerted, conscious effort. Skype, Google Hangouts, and other digital conferencing applications can help keep the team in touch and engaged.

Choose a reasonable schedule—biweekly or monthly, for example—and use it to welcome new team members and discuss project status, issues, and concerns. To help develop connections and enhance participation, including some fun, such as games or team-building exercises.

6. Make giving and receiving feedback and recognition a top priority.

Remote teams cannot participate in office milestones and achievement celebrations, and it can be difficult to give and receive feedback when you are unable to approach someone and congratulate them on a job well done.

On the other hand, numerous studies have shown that peer appreciation is a tremendous motivator for employees to achieve their best work. Remote teams can utilize collaboration technologies like Slack or purpose-built recognition and gamification platforms to deliver positive feedback, encouragement, and acknowledgment to one another in the absence of an in-person pat on the back.

Without the correct software solutions and tactics to keep team members interested, informed, and working efficiently, managing workflow across

Have No Fear, Remote Work Is Here!

remote teams may be cumbersome and complex. Workfront can provide a comprehensive, all-in-one platform to enable remote teams to stay connected, on task, and on time, no matter how dispersed they may be.

CHAPTER 3: WHAT LIES AHEAD

What is the future of remote working?

Remote employment has progressively increased in the two decades leading up to COVID-19, but it still accounts for a small percentage of the labor force. Companies frequently have no remote employees or severely restrict remote work, and the percentage of the workforce that was entirely remote was modest. In the pre-COVID Future Workforce survey, over half of employers said that none of their employees worked remotely for a substantial amount of the time. Only 2.3 percent of hiring managers had totally remote teams, and only 13.2 percent of the labor force represented worked entirely remotely. These modest figures are in line with prior projections.

Remote work has exploded in popularity, which is unsurprising. Before COVID-19, around half of recruiting managers dealt with remote talent in some capacity; today, that proportion has risen to 94 percent. The number of fully remote teams has also risen dramatically, from 2.3 percent to 20% in the post-COVID survey. Overall, the post-COVID survey results indicate that more than half of the workforce is now remote, which is in line with earlier research.

Have No Fear, Remote Work Is Here!

	Pre-COVID	Post-COVID
No remote workers on their team	46%	6%
Fully remote team	2.3%	20%
Share of their workers remote	13.2%	56% to 74%

(Alexander et al., 2021)

The Experiment with Remote Work

This rapid transition to remote teams is a novel experiment for most firms, and it represents a totally different way of working. Video chats have replaced face-to-face meetings, and a quick Slack message has replaced a brief visit to someone's desk or office.

While it's unsurprising that people have had to change how they work together since they're geographically separated, the poll shows that remote work is effective. Working remotely has gone better than predicted for 56 percent of recruiting managers, and it has gone as expected for another 35 percent. Only around one out of every ten times has it gone wrong.

Have No Fear, Remote Work Is Here!

While this survey result does not indicate whether remote work is going well or poorly - after all, it may be better than expected but still bad - it does show that the experiment is causing hiring managers to think more favorably about remote work in general. Furthermore, it would be remarkable if the 25% who said it went "far better than expected" did not mean it went extremely well.

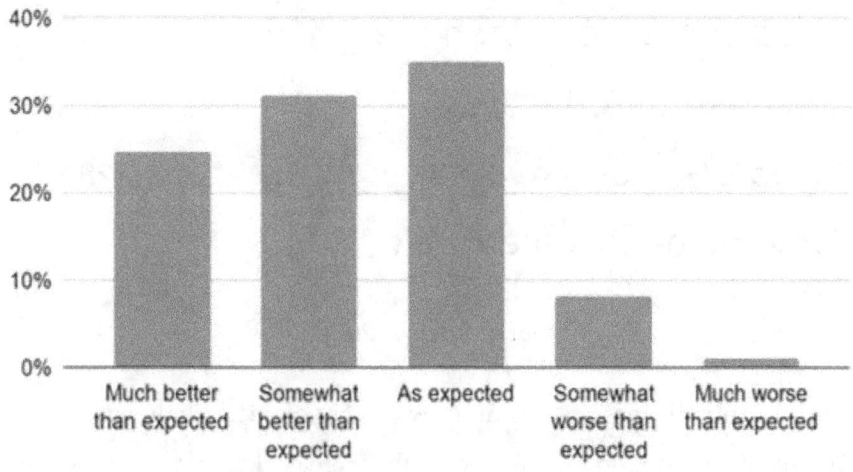

(Alexander et al., 2021)

The survey also allows one to learn more about why remote work is going so well.

The most popular responses for what has worked well with remote working were no commute, less non-essential meetings, and fewer office interruptions, all of which were shared by 40% or more respondents.

What, if anything, about remote work at your organization has worked well?	
No commute	49.0%
Reduction of non-essential meetings	46.3%
Less distractions than the office	41.2%
Increased productivity	32.2%
Greater autonomy	28.4%
Nothing has worked well	1.9%

(Alexander et al., 2021)

The most common reason for failure was technological challenges, which 36.2 percent of respondents agreed with. Increased distractions at home were the second most frequent response, with 32% of respondents. Importantly, the experience will lessen these two issues with remote employment. Because of the requirement to go remote quickly, many individuals and businesses adapt to new technology they have never used before, and many will need to experiment before settling on what works best for them. As technology advances, the number of people who find team cohesion, communication, and structure a challenge will undoubtedly decrease. Furthermore, while distractions at home are always a concern, the extensive closure of schools and restrictions on bringing help into the home during COVID-19 has almost definitely worsened this.

The most relevant finding is that 32.2 percent of hiring managers believe productivity has grown, while 22.5 percent believe it has declined. This bodes well for long-term adoption and the potential for remote labor to boost the economy's total productivity. Importantly, for overall U.S. productivity to rise due to remote work, it is not necessary for every job, or even the majority, to be more productive remotely; only some of them must be. Occupations that are more productive if done remotely will go remote over time, while less productive jobs will not. This selecting process will result in increased production as a result. Despite the quick speed of change and technological challenges, one-third of respondents believe remote work boosts productivity, which is a very encouraging sign for future adoption and productivity.

The future of remote work

What, if anything, about remote work at your organization has worked poorly?	
Technological issues	36.2%
Increased distractions at home	32.0%
Reduced team cohesion	30.5%
Difficulties in communication	30.3%
Teams are less organized	23.3%
Less productivity	22.5%
Nothing has worked poorly	14.8%

(Alexander et al., 2021)

In general, the survey findings show that the remote work experiment has gone better than predicted in terms of working conditions. There have been more benefits than drawbacks, and there is room for productivity improvement.

When respondents were asked how their workforce would change due to COVID-19, 26.3 percent indicated they would do much more remote work, and 35.6 percent said they would do slightly more, for a total of 61.9 percent planning more remote work.

By comparing a question addressed to hiring managers in the pre-and post-COVID survey waves, we may also peek into the medium-term future: In five years, what percentage of your whole team do you think will be working from home?

As a result of COVID-19, my organization's workforce will be...?	
Significantly more remote than it was before	26.3%
Somewhat more remote than it was before	35.6%
About the same as it was before	32.0%
Somewhat less remote than it was before	4.5%
Significantly less remote than it was before	1.6%

(Alexander et al., 2021)

Have No Fear, Remote Work Is Here!

According to the findings, many recruiting managers were already aiming to become more remote over the next five years, but this has increased dramatically. Before the COVID poll, 13.2 percent of the represented workforce worked totally remotely, with recruiting managers anticipating a 30 percent increase to 17.2 percent over the next five years. Following COVID, hiring managers expect 21.8 percent of their staff to be totally remote in five years, increasing 65 percent. The proportion of the workforce that is significantly remote is growing at a similar rate. In total, compared to what was envisaged before COVID-19, the expected rise of remote work has doubled.

	November, 2019	Five year forecasted rates		Five year growth	
		Pre-COVID	Post-COVID	Pre-COVID forecast	Post-COVID forecast
Entirely remote (all of their work is done remotely)	13.2%	17.2%	21.8%	30%	65%
Significantly remote (half or more of their time)	10.2%	13.7%	17.7%	33%	73%
Some remote (up to half of their time is spent remotely)	9.5%	15.0%	18.8%	57%	98%
Not at all remote (all of their work is done on-site or in-office)	67.1%	54.2%	41.7%	-19%	-38%

(Alexander et al., 2021)

According to the Future Workforce survey, the positive findings of the trial are expected to accelerate the trend of remote work even faster. Workers will benefit from the elimination of commutes, fewer meetings, and higher productivity due to this adjustment. Furthermore, suppose even a portion of those who are experimenting with remote work embrace it. In that case, it has the potential to quadruple the number of people working remotely and have a beneficial impact on staff productivity.

Recent Operating Issues of Working from Home

By directing projects and resources, business operations teams increase value and profitability. When entire teams must work remotely, however, the difficulties of working from home can stifle productivity and create a bottleneck in operations. On the other hand, the correct tools can aid in the resolution of many common concerns in operations management, as well as the particular issues that come with working from home.

Issues for Operations Management

Working at a distance is nothing new. Virtual teams, which include employees and supervisors worldwide, have become increasingly widespread in recent years. However, since the emergence of COVID-19, many organizations that previously collaborated in person have been compelled to adopt a work-from-home strategy — and many have made the switch permanent.

We have already discussed the major issues faced by operations management earlier. To remind you again they are

- Keeping track of performance.
- Communication.
- Scheduling.
- Developing Trust.
- The corporate culture.

Issues for Operations Team

Managers of operations aren't the only ones who struggle with working from home. Here are a few of the unique obstacles that employees of the operations team face when working remotely.

Organizing your work

Many remote workers struggle to prioritize their work without a morning briefing, pre-planned timetable, or in-person management to guide them. Furthermore, constant email updates and reminders might make it even more difficult for employees to choose where they should focus their attention.

Distractions and interruptions

The multitude of diversions and disruptions that can disrupt their focus and put a serious dent in productivity is perhaps the largest problem for professionals working from home. This can be an especially challenging transition for team members accustomed to working alongside their coworkers in the office, as coworkers tend to hold each other accountable when it comes to getting the job done.

Lack of face-to-face interaction

Working from home seems to be a dream come true for many employees until they understand how solitary it can be. For many employees, the office is more than just a place to work. Team members build ties, which can be difficult to deal with when they are suddenly unable to contact each other in person.

Reasons for Distributed Teams to Meet in Person

There are several reasons why meeting in person is beneficial; there are a few that you could predict and a couple that even surprised me.

Communication

While we frequently engage in video conversations with colleagues, we attempt to complete much of our work asynchronously because it can be difficult to organize time zones for a real-time meeting. This means that, depending on the colleague you're working with and how your time zones align, text is our major mode of contact. Chatting in Slack, discussing in Discourse, or simply adding comments to Dropbox Paper are all examples of "text."

Nonverbal clues, it turns out, influence 93 percent of communication success. With this in mind, speaking face to face becomes more crucial, which is why meeting your colleagues in person and working together may be quite beneficial.

I've discovered that after meeting in person, I work better with my teammates online. Even through the written word, I can imagine their tone and energy level, making the rest of our discussion go much more smoothly.

Brainstorming

Brainstorming is one of my favorite in-person professional activities. It can be difficult to brainstorm from afar. When everything happens asynchronously in a Paper doc, it can take a long time to get traction on a new concept. When there's an asynchronous debate going on in a Zoom video call, it can be tough to determine when to speak, thus two individuals often start talking at the same time, or other people don't speak at all because cutting in is difficult.

While we work on several exercises to clarify things up and make things easy for everyone, we still use in-person time at meetups to have lots of collaboration and brainstorming sessions. In person, brainstorming is extremely powerful for me, and making time for it has been a lot of pleasure over the years. It can be quite beneficial to brainstorm on issues such as the company's vision and values.

Increasing the Quality of Your Relationships

Several experiences can only be relieved in person. When we go to meetups, we frequently eat meals together, which has proven to be a very meaningful bonding experience. "People seated opposite one other unavoidably share dishes or pans, and are almost obliged to look each other in the eye and converse," according to one writer who investigated the matter.

While I've tried several online versions of journey sharing, nothing compares to seeing and feeling the emotions with the person sharing their experience across from you.

Touch

When we all get together in person, we tend to take over the space we're in (usually a hotel lobby) and spend a long time hugging and greeting each other. It's a pretty exciting aspect of the event, whether we're meeting for the first time or seeing a teammate after a year away! Physical contact, it turns out, is bringing us closer together.

Negotiators who shook hands were more open and honest and reached better outcomes, according to a study conducted by experts at the University of Chicago and Harvard University. It explained that the reward areas of the brain are activated when you shake your hands.

That implies all of our physical hugs throughout the week-long retreat are transmitting warmth to one another, which transfers over to the online realm as we relive the retreat together when we're all back in our cities.

How to Change from Pandemic Remote Work to Planned Remote Work

We are living in historically significant and game-changing times. The amenities we take for granted and our seemingly small gripes pale compared to the current climate, which has suddenly engulfed us all and to which we are slowly becoming acclimated. Most of us were compelled to work remotely due to COVID 19, which we call Pandemic Remote Work, however now most employers and employees are considering continuing to work remotely, which we call Planned Remote Work because it brings many benefits. However, based on my experience, here are a few recommendations for making planned remote work successful.

Develop a sense of trust

We've all heard about the general mocking of working from home productivity. Working from home, without question, has its drawbacks, but it also offers a great deal of flexibility. Here are a few ways for staying productive and avoiding distractions while building trust that will last well beyond this crisis and give you future flexibility:

- Create a daily schedule for yourself and agree on it with your family at home. Communicate this to your boss and agree on how to resolve any problems.

- Reevaluate your goals and objectives frequently – depending on the circumstances; key performance indicators may need to change to move focus to areas that produce impact. With your management, agree on a set of flexible deliverables. Spend 10 minutes at the start of each day writing a task list and crossing items off as you go. Communicate with your management weekly about your progress toward this goal.

- As leaders, listen to and discuss team members' routines and tasks and schedule calls to coincide with as many as feasible.

- Take advantage of the opportunity to slash some meetings. It's all too tempting to convert every meeting to an online format, but consider the specific goal and who is truly required. This will help to boost productivity for a long time to come.

- Encourage and share community and family support activities; everyone will feel more positive and involved.

- Employees must believe they're contributing value to the company, that the company values them, and that they may be happy working there.

<u>*Learn something*</u>

Although it is an important aspect of HR reviews and employee feedback, time for personal development is frequently lost in the day-to-day workplace environment and reduced to a form on the system. Once you've established your routines, set aside some time each week to learn something new that interests you. Here are a few options:

- Read (obviously) - choose a topic and, if you're unsure, ask colleagues and friends for recommendations on titles. You can also gather tips from online networks. Sit outside if the weather permits; otherwise, get as much vitamin D as possible by sitting near a window.

- Identify something that has historically taken up a lot of your time. Find a solution and present it to your larger team as an idea. Others are likely to feel the same way, and your improvements will have a long-term impact on business.

- Find an online course - it's fantastic to see so many businesses converting activities into free online courses on various subjects. YouTube is another excellent resource for finding a topic and learning from experts.

- Colleagues' brains — have brief, regular, mutually beneficial sessions with a coworker with a different skill set and share your experience. It will be wonderful to speak with someone, and it will also benefit your long-term collaboration.

<u>Believe in collaborations.</u>

In the current context, businesses can respond in one of two ways.

One option is to focus inward and only on your business interests, thereby cutting yourself off from anything that doesn't provide measurable value.

The other option is to form partnerships, which is the method I favor. Relationships when your experience aids a business in need, rather than standard commercial partnerships. Here is a list of some ideas for how to go about it:

- Offer your knowledge for free - it might be as easy as an online meeting, lesson, or course material to aid learning or provide advice to individuals who are in need.

- Create referral programmes to ensure that your free activities reach as many people as possible, as well as to test new partnerships that may prove commercially advantageous in the future.

- Make use of your demonstration equipment by determining how your items may assist someone at this time and putting them to good use. With so many events being cancelled, having your goods used rather than sitting in storage collecting dust is a far better option.

- Keep an open mind — while there may be no immediate commercial benefit, the assistance you provide today will be remembered and outlive this difficulty, assisting in developing your brand's credibility.

Learn about new technology.

Although it is nearly impossible to see beyond the near future, limitations will be lifted, and businesses will adapt to discover new methods to interact with customers and re-establish trust. There is now an opportunity to discover new, creative techniques that will help you stand out in the future business climate and reap the benefits. Here are some pointers on how to do so:

- Do your homework and choose items and services that you believe will help you achieve your long-term goals.

- Create your business case — implementing new internal processes can take a long time. Use this time to develop your plan, gather information, collaborate with vendors, and demonstrate your return on investment.

- Gain stakeholder buy-in by presenting your business case to your team and appropriate leadership to demonstrate your creative thinking and positive attitude toward moving the company ahead.

- As limitations ease, make sure your recommendations are included in all future planning sessions so that choices may be made swiftly.

How to Land a Remote Job

COVID 19 has taken a toll on practically everyone on the planet, causing drastic changes. With the current state of affairs, unemployment is at an all-time high, making it difficult to find a remote job or any other job for that matter. Almost everyone is looking for ways to make money on the internet. However, with such a high percentage of unemployment, there is also good growth in people eager to work online. I will teach you three main secrets that can help you acquire a remote job based on my personal experience.

SECRET #1: *Resume*

Every job application should include a résumé. An excellent resume is short, simple, and well-organized. When I say concise, I mean that all of your talents and accomplishments should fit on one piece of paper. Yes, this isn't a secret, but what can you do to get an employer to read your resume and immediately think, "Hey, this is exactly the kind of person I've been looking for." Now I'm going to start sharing my secrets.

An employer, after all, wants someone who understands his strengths and how they may help his company grow and generate more money. You must inform the employer how you may benefit him most enticingly and succinctly feasible. Assuring him that you can deliver is also important.

You can create a one-sentence pitch for yourself by following these three simple steps. Put what you can do to aid your target market and the results you can provide. "I assist virtual retailers in gaining more customers through my distinct and eye-catching advertising skills," for example.

And with that, I assure you that one of your employers will send you an email. Now look over your resume and make any necessary changes.

SECRET # 2: A broader range of specializations equals more career opportunities.

Employers want you more and are even prepared to pay you more if you specialize in your field. This also implies fewer competitors, resulting in a better chance of securing that job.

When you specialize in one talent, it simply means that you have mastered it and know all of the ins and outs of that particular job after doing it for a long time. This demonstrates to your company that you are capable of completing the work quickly and successfully.

I'm not joking when I say the higher pay rate. Employers now see you as a valuable asset to their organization, which implies you are entitled to a greater pay rate than the others. It will simply demonstrate how deserving you are based on your work performance.

SECRET #3: Become a member of a group.

This may be the most basic job-hunting strategy that most individuals are unaware of. It's important to remember that experts didn't start out as experts. They, too, began without knowing what to do and meeting challenges for which they had no answers, perhaps to the point where they simply hoped that their employer would not fire them for not doing a good job.

Believe me when I say that being in a group with others who did the same job as you is extremely beneficial. Quite a bit. You have someone you can rely on, or perhaps you can be that person for others. Everyone is eager to assist one another. Every achievement is lauded. It feels like you're developing as an individual while also collaborating with others in the community.

Where can you look for remote jobs?

It can be scary to consider working from home full-time or even travelling for an uncertain period of time and needing a flexible career. Fortunately, finding one is easier than you might think! As remote jobs become more prevalent, job boards respond by specializing in them. Here are a few sites:

1. We Work Remotely

This online job board allows job seekers to search for positions that are not limited by area, and it is updated regularly. To locate a career, you can start anywhere globally; simply search by title or skill. If you're a company trying to hire a remote worker, each post costs $200 for 30 days.

2. FlexJobs

FlexJobs is a job board for part-time, freelance, and remote workers, with 33k job ads from 4.6k organizations. The idea is for employees to have a "job that fits into your life, not a job that fits you in the life!"

3. Remote.co

Remote. co, which was founded by the same lady who founded FlexJobs, assists businesses in hiring, training, and managing remote workers. They provide an informative blog, as well as employee and employer Q&As and job listings.

4. Remote OK

Remote OK sends email alerts when new jobs in your category are posted, in addition to providing a daily listing of remote employment options. Though telecommuting professionals are most often employed in the technology area, Remote OK frequently posts job openings in other fields.

5. The Muse

The Muse, which bills itself as the "ultimate career discovery and counselling website," provides behind-the-scenes access to on-site and virtual work prospects. You can look for employment by specifying a location (remote) and keywords, or you can look into the culture of a firm that recruits remote workers if you know one.

6. Upwork

This website, which is more of a community for employers and job seekers, allows businesses to offer freelance work and hire those who apply. It's a terrific way to get your side hustle on without having to commit to coming to an office, even if it's not full-time. What's the catch? Upwork charges a service fee depending on the client's billing method, but you can get hired and paid quickly!

7. Indeed

Simply type "remote" in the "where" column to use our massive job board to find a remote position. You may also upload your resume to help employers find you if they're seeking remote workers.

CHAPTER 4: EMPLOYEE PRECISION

How to write a job description for remote jobs

A well-written job description is a crucial aspect of a job posting that may do wonders for your firm. Well-chosen terms clarify what the job entails and eliminate any potential for misunderstanding. A well-written job description can also aid your recruiting and retention efforts by attracting and retaining the top personnel.

Writing a job description entails more than just outlining the role's core work tasks and identifying a salary range. An effective job description encompasses nearly all of an employee's responsibilities, informing applicants of what they must accomplish, how they must do it, and how their performance will be judged.

Writing a job description for a job posting is similar in certain ways, whether the position is remote or in-person. However, not everyone is suited to working from home. It's critical to include numerous remote-specific components in your job description if you want to attract and retain top remote workers.

Job Description Writing

Ensure you include some of the fundamental parts of any job description before writing your remote job description.

Short and to the point

The information regarding the role in a job posting should be dynamic and exciting. Job postings are essentially an advertisement for the position you're looking to fill. To persuade suitable applicants to apply for the position, you should make the job and the firm sound exciting or desirable.

That said, you don't want to simply declare, "It's a cool job," and go on. You want to make sure that applicants have a good understanding of what the position entails. You don't have to go in-depth about the role. You should, however, include aspects that will help employees grasp their core responsibilities, what will be expected of them, and what the outcome looks like.

Use a Unique Title

Although having the title of "Rockstar Marketer" or "People Wizard" is entertaining, these aren't especially useful or clear job titles. While these titles may make your organization appear to be a fun place to work, they have little meaning outside of your workplace.

If you use that job title in a job posting, at the very least, the people you want will have a difficult time locating it. Few people have a degree in "People Wizarding," thus it's unlikely that job seekers are looking for a People Wizard position while they're looking for new employment. Traditional job titles like "Human Resources Specialist" or "Human Resources Coordinator" are more frequent.

Stick to typical job names that people are likely looking for when writing the job description. As a result, your job ad is more likely to appear in their search results.

Use Language That Is Inclusive

Make sure you're not using any gendered language in your job description, other than utilizing gender-neutral language (salesperson instead of salesman or saleswoman). Using gender-neutral wording throughout your job description will help you attract a more diverse pool of candidates.

According to one study, utilizing male terminology in job advertising and descriptions (Ninja, Confident, Hacker, Rockstar) can make women less likely to fit into the job or organization. While masculine-worded job descriptions did not affect a woman's perception of the degree of abilities required for the job, they may discourage women from applying.

Naturally, you want employees who are self-assured and determined. You'll probably also want people who are dedicated and work well together. Keep in mind that to encourage every competent candidate to apply, you may need to balance masculine adjectives with an equal number of feminine words (i.e., Collaborative, Committed, Cooperative)

Combine the sour and the sweet

While it's easy to focus on the positive aspects of the position in a job description, it's not fair to leave out potential deal-breakers—factors that could influence whether or not someone accepts the offer.

For example, if the position demands a lot of travel outside of the country, make sure to mention it in the job description. You don't want someone in a position where they despise traveling or can't stay away from home for long periods. It's better to admit the less desirable features of a job upfront than wait until it's time to make an offer and find out the person isn't interested because you left out an "essential detail."

How to Write a Job Description for a Remote Position

While a virtual job description contains much of the same information as a traditional job description, you should include some remote-specific features.

Because you only want to interview people who want to work from home, make it obvious that this is a remote position. You also want those who wish to work from home to be able to find your job posting. To ensure that this occurs, make it clear that this is a remote location.

Make Use of the Appropriate Remote Keywords

In the same way that you should include often searched job names in your job description, you should employ frequently searched remote keywords. Using the correct remote terminology in the job description helps applicants understand that the position is remote, and it helps your job search appear in the search results of people looking for remote jobs.

Consider including any of the following popular remote keywords in your job description:

- Working from home.
- Remote.
- Distributed.
- Work from anywhere.
- Virtual.
- Office at home.

Define the term "flexible"

When it comes to work hours, many remote jobs allow you some flexibility. However, this does not always imply that employees can work whenever they wish. If your human resource department's remote work policy requires employees to be "on" during specific hours, make that clear in the job description.

If someone must work between 10 a.m. and 2 p.m. Eastern Time, specify it in the job description. If you don't, you can discover that staff is scarce during that period, making team meetings and client business impossible to conduct.

Define the term "remote"

Just because you provide remote work doesn't imply your employees will work from home all of the time. You might need them to come into the office for meetings or training a couple of days a week. Similarly, a position may be remote during the pandemic, but then transition to in-office employment once the situation has stabilized.

Define what remote means now and in the future for the role. Determine what happens to the role if it is required to be remote during the epidemic. When things get back to normal, will individuals be able to work from home again? Will, there be five days in the workplace again, or only a few? If the remote part of the position is only temporary, ensure its stated explicitly in the job description so there's no confusion afterward.

Make the location clear.

A typical misperception regarding remote employment is that one may work for a remote company from anywhere; however, this is not always the case. Many remote enterprises (and roughly 95% of remote jobs!) have location requirements. Employees at some companies are allowed to work from home, but they must reside close to the office for meetings or be near the client base.

Specify where someone must live while they work remotely for you for whatever reason. You may also need to explain why someone needs to live in a specific area in some situations. If it's for clients, make it clear. Alternatively, if it's to attend weekly meetings regularly, mention that as well.

Specify the location of the work.

Your remote function may have additional location requirements outside a country or state. Someone working with sensitive personal information, for example, may not be permitted to work from a coffee shop. You may not want employees accessing your servers from a public Wi-Fi connection, even if the work isn't sensitive.

Mention any location criteria that aren't limited to a city or state, along with an explanation of why. "You must work from your home office because you will be managing confidential client information. You are not permitted to work in a public place (such as a coffee shop or a library)."

Describe your tools.

Be explicit about the technology that your employees require. Do they necessitate a specific type of computer? What about internet speed or a virtual private network (VPN)? Describe all of the equipment that the company will offer to the employee and any technical assistance or equipment stipends that you provide to virtual workers.

If you want staff to use their equipment, make sure to specify it in the job description. Define which software programs individuals will utilize as well. Even though many things are now cloud-based, you may still need particular licenses for your employees to use these products. Determine what they should have and who will be responsible for paying for it.

Mention the Meetings

Some remote organizations hold mandated all-company meetings once or twice a year. While some jobs provide more flexibility and control over daily schedules, employees may still be required to be on call at particular times. Although flexible employment allows workers to set their hours, there may still be meetings held on X Day and Y time.

Make certain that these mandatory meetings are included in the job description. However, you are not required to include exact days and hours. "Must attend weekly department meetings" or "Required to attend business retreat twice a year" are simple examples.

Discuss the Interview

In certain ways, a job interview is a job interview, regardless of the type of work. Virtual interviews for remote positions, on the other hand, are frequently distinct from in-person interviews for in-office jobs. Aside from the pandemic, you should plan out the interview process.

Consider whether you'll employ video conferencing or whether the candidate will be required to visit your virtual office platform. It's also OK if you communicate via phone. Just make sure you mention this crucial step in the process.

Metrics to Ensure that You've Hired the Best Remote Worker

Focus on these four indicators to get the most out of your monitoring efforts.

1. Productivity

Productivity is a simple yet complex metric that both employees and managers should consider before implementing a monitoring strategy. Assessing productivity is as crucial as ensuring a reasonable workday as it is about holding disengaged employees accountable. Consider switching to an outcomes-based approach to productivity, in which micro targets and other product-based goals are used as the optimum productivity measures. Most people aspire to be good at their jobs, and success isn't always measured in hours spent in front of a computer screen.

2. Participation and Collaboration

Employees require greater communication with management and coworkers than ever before during this particularly trying period. While there appears to be a limitless number of communication venues, their combined effect is frequently the same. Zoom fatigue exists, and it isn't the answer to empowering employees to succeed. On the other hand, morning and lunchtime check-ins can help employees stay connected to the organization and each other. Monitoring software generates communication metrics that can be used to analyze everyone's commitment to communication and employee happiness and productivity.

3. Trends in Big Data

While focused monitoring can feel intrusive and overwhelming, big data trends can offer crucial information about best practices in workflow, office norms, and potential bottlenecks.

Many people are open to learning about big data trends that can lead to significant behavioral changes.

This could have ramifications such as:

- Communication best practices and conventions.

- High-frequency work periods and customer involvement.

- Work habits and expected results.

- Typical productivity stumbling blocks.

Big data is driving workplace trends across the board, but when used too precisely, it can backfire.

4. Cybersecurity

The cybersecurity landscape for remote workers is complex, posing a threat to both personal and company data. Employ employee monitoring tools in this context to track employee participation about common hazards, like phishing schemes, and to provide real-time training in best practices. This programme can also detect and defend against insider attacks. It may provide everyone with a deeper awareness of the hazards while also offering the tools needed to secure their information as an evaluation metric.

KPIs to Measure the Performance of Remote Workers

The first thing to remember about KPIs is that they aren't supposed to function like Sauron's Eye. KPIs aim to bring your entire staff on board, grasp the company's goals, and establish clear expectations. Visual reporting systems can help staff stay on track by turning KPIs into appealing diagrams and graphs, but they don't indicate the quality of the work done. Your team will withdraw and hide if numbers and colours are constantly reminding them that they aren't accomplishing enough or if you use reports as a pretext to check on them ten times a day.

3 Things to Remember When Using KPI Metrics

Tracking software that displays metrics in real-time to each department of your team is the greatest way to assess remote workers' productivity. As previously said, the goal of KPIs is to track productivity without sacrificing product or delivery quality. Keep these three things in mind when reviewing your team's metrics:

Performance of Team Members

Deadlines are crucial, and everyone must adhere to them. It is not just a matter of time, but also of quality, how each team member produces their final output. Metrics that track employee performance can assist you in coordinating activities with other departments and establishing objectives. Of course, this does not negate that it is inconvenient if someone consistently takes a week longer than expected. Without putting your team members under stress, the software can help you spot red flags, burnout, and areas for improvement in overall performance.

Communication

You can then monitor internal communication once you have an overview of your team member's performance. A trustworthy reporting technique is required to coordinate multiple departments working on the same goal in virtual teams. Updating shared documents and data is just as important as accomplishing duties, and everyone in the company should have access to them. Of course, this doesn't mean that you must send out thousands of reminders or hold weekly video conferences and meetings to assess engagement and communication. The goal of transparent reporting is to keep track of what has been done to improve cross-departmental communication. Observing what others are doing allows more realistic requests to be communicated and internal conflict to be avoided.

Learning Ability

The learning mindset is the last factor to consider when evaluating your team's performance. Keeping up with the latest trends and technologies is more important than ever before for productivity and goals. A bottleneck is indicated when delivery is slow, or communication is difficult because some of your staff refuse to adjust to new tools. Use this factor to determine whether you need to make changes to your system or team.

Have No Fear, Remote Work Is Here!

How to Evaluate the Performance and Accountability of Virtual Employees

Keep it short and focused on aligning common goals when defining a KPI for your remote workforce. Timelines and achievability are important indications that everyone can follow. Your marketing team doesn't need to master programming languages to see how the development team is performing. You should think of KPIs as your team's language, which everyone speaks to help work go as smoothly as possible.

This is what you should think about for your team's productivity:

Accountability: Working from home does not imply complete independence or isolation. Each team member must take responsibility and contribute and assist even if they are far away.

Self-discipline and Integrity: Because remote workers have less direct supervision, it's critical to think about how they'll arrange and prioritize duties over time.

Adaptability to Remote Work Experience: how well your staff adapts to working from home and growing comfortable with it.

Establish a Work from Home Policy: It's critical to track how your employees stick to your policy over time to see if they suit your company's culture and goals.

Taking a Self-Assessment

KPIs aren't just for gauging the efficiency of your virtual staff. In virtual teams, performance metrics are especially important for keeping track of mistakes and low-performing methods. These numbers aren't there, so you can point the finger at your personnel.

They're there to help you learn, change, and increase your productivity. Measuring using new technology isn't a way to shame your remote workers; it's a way to ensure that they have a better experience and are more productive. Measuring the satisfaction of your team members is critical for improving workflow and team structure. Include a metric in your KPIs that allows your workforce to communicate their feelings regarding your company's policies.

In virtual teams, for example, mental health is a major concern. Although remote workers are more productive and have a better work-life balance, it might be difficult for some to put their laptops away at night. KPIs let you keep track of your team's personal and professional lives, as well as any potential distractions that slow down delivery.

It will be easier to establish a solid workflow and team chemistry if your remote workers are satisfied with your company policies. Remote workers are still part of a team, and a tight-knit group makes onboarding new members and launching new initiatives easier. It's also easy to imagine the perfect personality fit for your team with a clear structure of jobs and responsibilities.

That is your primary worry. Because of your wonderful virtual workforce, the quality of your products and productivity will improve, not because of software measurements!

How to Give Your Employees the Right Training for Remote Work

The necessity for remote employee training is urgent, owing to the COVID-19 problem, which has put it at the forefront. Many public and commercial companies have been compelled to implement a remote training approach with little or no planning or lead time.

Create a work-at-home handbook: It's all about information, but it's also about retention. To ensure that everyone in your company is on the same page during this crisis, establish a guide to go whenever they need it. It could be in the form of a PDF file, a video, or an online course. Just make sure it's a simple, step-by-step instruction that explains how to work from home while remaining productive.

Provide purpose and value training: Inquire of anyone who works from home full-time. They'll all acknowledge that remote work can feel like "no work" at times. Detaching someone from a group of individuals working on the same goal can cause them to lose sight of the goal. So, to keep your staff motivated, you must teach them about your company's vision and values. During their onboarding, 61 percent of employees report their employers provided them with no training on corporate culture. If your company is one of those, teaching your employees about the culture before going remote sounds like a good idea.

Online training: Although face-to-face training may not be possible, you must not allow this to deter you from pursuing your training goals. You may always conduct online training if you and your team are forced to work from home due to unforeseen circumstances. If an LMS designed for staff training appears to be too difficult at this time, you can start with a simpler option. Create web movies that your employees can watch from the comfort of their home office, or create a shared folder to keep all material in one place by using a video conferencing platform.

Train how to use technology: Remote working comes with a set of tools that employees must become familiar with. The list goes on and on with communication apps, collaboration tools, video conferencing software, and so on. It may be too much for some.

Include important skills in your training: It's critical now to enable people to execute their jobs just as well – if not better – from home. This will necessitate a separate set of abilities, including:

Management of time and distractions: Not all employees can work at home with the same discipline as those who work on-site. Even if you schedule work hours, communicate ideas, and use tools to avoid distractions and wasted time – such as noise-canceling headphones, shutting off device alerts, and following deep work tactics - they may not be able to focus when they need to.

Etiquette in communication: The majority of employees aren't used to just communicating with coworkers on the internet. Some people utilize apps and technology they've never used before. As a result, the same old communication and social rules no longer apply. Go over the basic functionalities of all your platforms in remote work training. Create an etiquette guide with video, chat, email, and phone conversation guidelines and put it online. Include instructions on:

- Appropriate hours for communications to be sent and responses to be expected.

- The appropriate avenues for communication (for example, use video conference to make final decisions, chat to share documents, email to send information before the meeting, etc.)

- Appropriate videoconferencing clothes and setting, and anticipate continued collegiality and professionalism on all channels.

Access to resources and information: In a situation, employees on-site frequently looked to their coworkers for assistance. They'll have to fend for themselves at home in terms of IT, research, and implementation. So teach or retrain your personnel how to use your accessible systems and troubleshoot common IT issues. Provide them with tip sheets on what's in your databases and how to access and traverse them independently.

Have No Fear, Remote Work Is Here!

Go for the approach that best suits your needs: Remote training, like in-person training, cannot be a one-size-fits-all solution. Reading and reviewing might help some employees absorb everything. Others will require video education and interaction in real-time.

<u>Here are some strategies to consider:</u>

Learning in real-time: This can be done using synchronous channels like Zoom, a conference call, or a cloud-based, computer-linked session, such as LogMeIn. As information is shared, everyone (or just one) learns. It's as close to classroom training as you can get. However, you must plan ahead of time to ensure that everyone is available for the session.

Self-directed learning: Employees can access learning information whenever they choose, then remark, participate in activities, and/or take assessments according to the deadlines. However, you'll need a constantly updated collection of training material for employees to benefit from, including anything from documents and exams to video and software.

Blended learning: It is a term that refers to a method of learning. This hybrid of real-time and self-directed learning caters to a wide range of learners and learning situations. It's great for intricate training, but it's too time-consuming for quick-hit, urgent training.

Have No Fear, Remote Work Is Here!

Top Virtual Instructor-Led Training Platforms

A facilitator teaches a remote training class through a virtual learning platform or software in virtual instructor-led training (VILT). VILT creates a synchronous remote learning environment in which users can communicate and study together in real-time.

I went through many VILT hosting platforms and came up with a list of the top 5 most popular VILT hosting platforms.

1. Zoom.
2. Google Meet.
3. Microsoft Teams.
4. Webex.
5. Adobe Connect.

What Is Virtual Instructor-Led Training, and How Does It Work?

When a facilitator leads a remote training class using a virtual learning platform or software, it is known as virtual instructor-led training (VILT). VILT is synchronous, collaborative, and takes place in real-time over a digital platform, similar to traditional instructor-led training (ILT).

VILT can be manifested in a variety of ways, including:

Webinar - A webinar usually consists of one facilitator and several participants. Polling, voting, or video conferencing may be required of students.

1:1 - There is one facilitator and one participant, similar to peer-to-peer training.

Small-Group - A virtual classroom setting with 3-5 participants and one facilitator is commonly used to learn new processes or tasks.

Lecture - A lecture is a big group of learners led by a single facilitator.

Workshop - Participants gather in a workshop to learn new software or activity through hands-on training. Learners can go away and practice on their own, with additional homework or a follow-up session later.

Virtual Classroom - Learners are muted and merely watch the facilitator navigate the exercise in a virtual classroom, similar to a lecture.

Many organizations are faced with changing their current ILT programme into VILT in light of the COVID-19 epidemic. To do so, businesses must alter their existing programmes to accommodate the new normal of a remote workforce.

Zoom

Date of Release: 2012

Characteristics:

- Rooms for private meetings.

- Backgrounds that are not real.

- Integration with the calendar.

- Room for waiting.

- Multi-screen collaboration.

- Make-up application.

Have No Fear, Remote Work Is Here!

- By dialing a phone number, you can join.

Business Plan: $199 per license per year

Zoom has a maximum capacity of 500 participants.

Users: Zoom had over 300 million daily meetings hosted on their platform as of April 2020.

Zoom is a cloud-based peer-to-peer software platform that delivers video telephony and online chat services for teleconferencing, telecommuting, distance education, and social contacts.

Google Meet

Characteristics:

- Video conferencing for businesses.

- Video calls and messaging that are encrypted.

- Google Workspace integration.

- captions in real-time.

- Cancellation of noise.

- By dialing a phone number, you can join.

As part of a Google Workspace Plan, standard business is $8 per month per user.

Maximum Capacity: Up to 250 people can use Google Workspace Enterprise.

Number of Users: Google Meet had almost 100 million daily users last year.

Google Meet, formerly known as Hangouts Meet, allows teams and organizations to hold secure video meetings. Participants can share their screens, raise their hands, join breakout rooms, and participate in surveys and Q&A sessions.

Microsoft Teams

Date of Release: 2017

Characteristics:

- File storage and screen sharing.

Have No Fear, Remote Work Is Here!

- Integration of applications.

- Access is restricted.

- Other devices can be linked to.

- Meeting recordings and notes should be shared.

- Rooms for discussion.

Basic Plan for Microsoft 365 Business Monthly fee: $5 per user

Maximum Capacity: Office 365 E3 can accommodate up to 10,000 users.

Number of Users: Microsoft Teams had 115 million daily active users as of October 2020.

It is a collaboration platform for businesses that is part of the Microsoft 365 suite of products. Users may host video conferences, virtual events, and voice conferencing with Microsoft Teams.

<u>WebEx</u>

Date of Release: 1996

Characteristics:

- Speech improvement and noise reduction.

- Emojis that appear on the screen.

- Translation in real-time.

- Meeting templates can be used to present content as a personal meeting background.

- Calls to meetings transition.

Price per month for the Business Plan: $26.95 per host

Maximum Capacity: The Business Plan may accommodate up to 200 people.

WebEx had over 100 million daily conference participants in May of 2020.

Cisco's WebEx allows users to video conference and meet online with anyone in the world over a secure connection, with HD video and audio, screen sharing features, group messaging, and more.

Adobe Connect

Date of Release: 2019

Characteristics:

- Whiteboards, polls, and Q&A.

- Pods, layouts, and bespoke branding provide advanced customization choices.

- Access is restricted.

- Annotations and drawings.

Meetings with Adobe Connect Monthly fee is $50.

Maximum Attendance: Adobe Connect Webinars may accommodate up to 1000 people.

Adobe Connect has over 2.5 million users and 15,000 customers throughout the world since its introduction.

Adobe Connect is a modern VILT, web conferencing, and webinar hosting software. Adobe Connect was once a component of the Adobe Acrobat family, and it went by numerous different names, including Presedia Publishing System and Adobe Acrobat Connect Pro.

How to Tackle Disciplinary Issues in Remote Work Environments

There's no need to put off a disciplinary or grievance process just because employees are working remotely. Employers must, however, assess whether a thorough and impartial investigation of the issues can be conducted while working under lockdown conditions.

If significant records or documentation cannot be collected due to the workplace being closed, or if key witnesses cannot be interviewed due to practical obstacles, it may be more equitable to postpone the resolution of the procedure until this evidence can be obtained. On a case-by-case basis, this will have to be decided.

Many companies have undoubtedly dealt with this issue, and they will continue to do so in the future. Disciplinary issues will continue to exist and need to be addressed; nevertheless, an employer will have additional concerns.

Be Open and Transparent

The first thing that should be a must is to consider the safety and health of all personnel participating in the process, including witnesses and the individual in question. Before determining whether to pause or invoke the disciplinary procedure, you must be open and candid with these persons, listening to their concerns. In the context of Covid-19, you'll need to assess if you'll be able to discover a fair, reasonable, and safe means to carry it out. You should be honest with them and explain how you intend to conduct inquiry meetings and any following disciplinary hearings remotely. Whatever you determine should be communicated to those involved in writing. Furthermore, suppose any of the employees engaged are on leave. In that case, any participation in the process will need to be carefully considered, given the limits imposed on them by the Coronavirus Job Retention Scheme.

Investigate

If you decide to go ahead with your disciplinary proceedings, any investigation must, of course, be conducted fairly. You've stated that you'd like to conduct your investigation interviews and any following disciplinary hearings via videoconference. If that's the case, you'll need to consider if everyone involved, including witnesses, can access video equipment and an internet connection. Consider whether anyone involved is disabled and what reasonable accommodations could be required. Whether it's an investigation meeting or a disciplinary hearing, you'll need to make sure that all aspects of it can be carried out properly and fairly, including witness testimony, how you'll introduce documents and have them considered, and how you'll handle any cross-examination of witnesses in a disciplinary hearing.

Be Considerate

Remember that even if the disciplinary hearing is conducted remotely, the right to be accompanied will still apply. If the companion cannot attend, you must allow the employee to recommend a different day and time, as long as it is convenient and not more than five working days after the original hearing date. If an employee requests a longer duration because their companion is unavailable, think about if you should grant it. It's worth noting that the right to challenge any decision will remain in place, and any appeal procedure must be followed, taking into account the same additional considerations outlined above.

Assess

Suppose you file a claim with the Employment Tribunal. In that case, the Employment Tribunal will assess whether you followed your processes in a reasonable, balanced, and fair manner, as well as the impact of the Covid-19 pandemic. If you're unsure about how to proceed, I recommend seeking legal assistance as soon as possible.

Tips for Team Building in a Remote Environment

Try to incorporate as many of these team-building events as possible for your remote employees:

Have No Fear, Remote Work Is Here!

1. Host virtual chats weekly.

Consider organizing brief weekly or bi-weekly video chats with your team so that everyone can share updates on non-work-related topics such as weekend plans or popular TV chit-chat.

Employees can make eye contact, catch up on facial or emotional cues, and interact as if conversing in person by having everyone on camera via video chat. When communicating off-camera in the future, it also helps put a face to everyone's email or screen aliases.

2. Create a Slack channel dedicated to team building.

Separate Slack channels for non-work-related conversations facilitate this. It's as easy as creating and naming different channels depending on a single subject, such as funny memes. This keeps your legitimate work chats from becoming overrun with kitten videos.

Include a description of each channel in your remote working policy, as well as a brief explanation about how to use these chats without being distracted.

3. Participate in the Appropriate Games.

The correct team activities provide a fun and participatory way to break up the monotony of your remote employees' daily routines.

Consider the following suggestions:

Guess who that teeny-tiny employee is: Request that everyone sent in a newborn photo or a snapshot of themselves when they were younger. Each week, choose one employee and have the rest of the team guess who it is. This should keep you laughing for a few months on #ThrowbackThursdays.

Quizzes: Use fascinating information about your team or pop culture trivia in a fast quiz or inquiry. Give a small prize or reward to the person who gets the correct answers.

Two truths and a lie: In this game, someone must communicate three statements with the others, and they must guess which one is false.

Weekly caption/snap share contest: Request that each team member contributes their favorite shot from the previous week. Ask everyone else to caption the shot with a snappy one-liner to ramp up the effect.

Virtual games like Words with Friends bring your team together while also providing a challenge for everyone.

<u>**4. Organize a virtual movie or television show night**</u>

To do so, use a group video chat to broadcast your movie or TV show (Game of Thrones, The Office, or Jeopardy! anyone?) Then everyone may watch at the same time and remark in real-time in the chatbox. This is a one-of-a-kind technique to bring people together. It's an excellent remote team-building activity because it doesn't necessitate a lot of extra effort or money.

5: Schedule quarterly or annual retreats in exotic locales.

Bringing everyone together for a retreat is one of the most effective methods to foster teamwork. Bonus points if you choose an exotic location to which everyone quickly RSVPs. Plan a few team-building events and leave the rest of the schedule open for adventures and relaxation.

Despite the cost, having a weekend retreat will be well worth it when everyone returns to work refreshed, connected, and ready to attack your goals as one well-oiled machine.

Virtual Team Building Exercises

Remote teams have fewer opportunities to mingle, making it difficult for members to get to know one another. This can lead to feelings of loneliness and alienation from our coworkers and team conflict, and lower productivity.

Remote teams might benefit from virtual team-building exercises to overcome these challenges and foster a feeling of community and shared understanding.

Have No Fear, Remote Work Is Here!

Organizing a Virtual Team-Building Activity

Begin by identifying your goals and objectives. Do you wish to improve your project management or negotiation skills, for example? The goal of your team-building exercise should be to achieve your goal while also encouraging individual and team growth.

Calculate how much time you have for each activity while planning your exercises. Problem-solving tasks that need collaboration will take longer than "ice breakers."

Consider the participants' cultural expectations as well as their particular characteristics. Introverts may find it difficult to speak up in group conversations. If they work from home, they may potentially be experiencing overstimulation. Extroverts, on the other hand, may tend to dominate. Allow adequate time for introductions because some members of your team may not have met before. Use short, amusing Virtual Icebreakers to get people talking if they don't know one another. Also, think about different ways people can contribute so that everyone has a say.

Five Team-Building Exercises for Virtual Teams

Let's have a look at some team-building exercises you may do with your team remotely. They're made to help your team communicate better, create trust, improve listening skills, and gain a deeper understanding of one another.

1. Four Facts and a Fib

This activity is perfect for a group of people who don't know each other very well. It requires a casual setting for people to discuss personal information and establish trust.

People and Materials

Suitable for any size group. A pen and paper are required for each participant.

Time

Depending on the size of the group, allow roughly 20 minutes for completion.

Instructions

Request that the participants write down five "facts" about themselves, one of which must be a lie - but credible one. "I once swam with dolphins," rather than "I wrestled a shark!"

Allow adequate time for participants to jot down their facts. When they're done, go around the room and have each person read out their five facts. Guess which facts about each person are true and which are false as a group. Discuss the results after each person has shared their facts and lies.

Were there any surprises? If yes, did the truths surprise you more than the lie?

2. Escape Room

A themed challenge event in which players collaborate to collect clues, accomplish tasks, and solve various riddles is known as an Escape Room. It has the potential to enhance communication, teamwork, and decision-making abilities.

People and Materials

Escape room games are usually designed for groups of three to six people and take a lot of creativity in order to play them. In fact, using a third-party vendor is frequently more convenient.

Time

The standard scenario involves escaping within a certain amount of time, generally an hour.

Instructions

Instructions vary for each game and can include things like codebreaking, word games, and math puzzles.

3. Origami for the Blind

The goal of this activity is to emphasize the value of listening and soliciting feedback.

People and Materials

- Virtual pairs of any number of persons.

- Phone or texting app (no video).

- Each person will need a page of Letter or A4 paper.

Time

Time is approximately 25 to 30 minutes.

Instructions

Origami instructions will be emailed to one individual from each pair. These can be found on a variety of hobby websites. Take a look at origame.me, for example.

The individual who has the instructions should use a messaging or video conferencing software to walk their partner (the receiver) through the steps of making an origami construction (but with the camera turned off).

During the call, the receiver can ask questions, request clarification, and provide comments. Participants can turn their cameras back on once each group has finished observing if the receiver got the origami building correct.

4. Scrabble

This entertaining practice is intended to stimulate creative thinking, promote teamwork, and improve communication. It works well with virtual meeting software like Zoom, allowing teams to divide into virtual breakout rooms.

People and Materials

This is best done in groups of 12 or more people. You'll need a bag of Scrabble tiles, as well as pens and paper for the participants.

Time

Allow 20 minutes to complete the task.

Instructions

Each person should be given two or three letters at random. Then, at random, divide the group into teams. The practice will be most effective if each team has six to nine persons. In 10 minutes, have each group come up with as many words as possible using their letters. Before you begin, go over the following guidelines with the group:

- Each letter tile can only be used once per word.

- Three or more letters are required in words.

- Plurals of a word that have previously been used are not permitted. For instance, you can have either "tree" or "trees," but not both.

- Proper names, such as place names or forenames, are not permitted.

- If desired, each side can switch up to two of their letters before the game begins.

Three-letter words earn two points, four-letter words earn three points, and so on. A five-point bonus is awarded to the longest word.

5. Lost at Sea

Decision-making, cooperation, and critical thinking are all emphasized in this activity.

People and Materials

Approximately five or six individuals in each team. Each participant will require a separate copy of a worksheet.

Time

Time is flexible, but try to keep it between 25 and 40 minutes.

Instructions

Give your team members the scenario of being shipwrecked at sea with only a few items. They must rank the objects according to how valuable they would be in assisting the group's survival. They should work on their initiative, then as a group.

Participants should be divided into teams, and everyone should be given a ranking sheet.

Step 1: Give each team member 10 minutes to rank the things in order of significance on their own. This should be done in the sheet's second column.

Step 2: Allow the teams 10 minutes more to confer and settle on their group rankings. They should write them down in the third column of their papers once they've agreed.

Step 3: Have each group compare their ranks to the group's overall rankings and think about why any scores differ.

Step 4: Now read aloud the "proper" order, as compiled by the US Coast Guard's specialists. These should be added to the sheet by the participants.

Step 5: Have the teams think about why they made their decisions and compare their results to the experts' recommendations.

How to Determine Remote workers' Salaries

Salaries for traditional jobs requiring a physical presence in an office are often determined after a business analysis of a data set. One of the most crucial elements being investigated is how much other workers in the same field in the company's immediate vicinity are paid.

Following are the major factors that should be kept in mind when determining remote salaries:

<u>**1. The Company's Location and Salary Structure**</u>

Salaries are calculated using an average of around 70% of the market and are exclusively based on the obligations of the job at a certain level. If a telecommuter works in an expensive city, they are given some leeway. Overall, salaries are determined regardless of the location of the remote worker. Typically, the barometer is set between a more expensive and a less expensive region.

On the other hand, a telecommuter living in a high-priced neighborhood may get paid simply based on the location of the company's headquarters. If it's in a less expensive neighborhood, you can get paid less. Other businesses may make decisions based on the national average. Some employers just demand the same wage regardless of where a stay-at-home employee is situated when hiring remote workers.

2. Salaries and Workplaces for Remote Workers

Having employees in a high-cost metro area while others work in different locations can be beneficial if a company understands how to calculate compensation based on the location of remote workers appropriately. When their location determines a remote worker's wage, a person working from home in San Francisco will need a different salary than someone working in Kansas City, Missouri. As a result, when assessing pay based on a worker's location rather than the company's location, flexibility is required. Employers of work-at-home employees should regularly get familiar with the local, state, and national laws in their employees' locations to decide whether employment rules and regulations apply.

3. Market Trends Influence Salaries Regardless of Location

Companies in a mid-sized city may decide that "comparing what they give in terms of the salary plus benefits and other allowances of an in-office employee in the same market" is the best way to determine a remote employee's salary."

Companies compensate stay-at-home workers for the work they accomplish with this method. The pace is quite constant and isn't substantially affected by a worker's location. Salary figures are calculated based on a variety of job-related parameters. No matter how much the company pays or where their city is located globally, these telecommuters tend to be on the outskirts of major cities. In most cases, firms will provide extras such as bonuses, which can significantly increase a person's wages. Regardless, each job has a set salary range.

Primary Approaches to Remote Salaries

When it comes to paying a decent salary to remote employees, there are three primary possibilities, having their own advantages and drawbacks. Again, there is no simple solution to this problem and no true one-size-fits-all approach that every business should take. Instead, think about the options available to you and how they fit your company's pay philosophy and employee retention plan.

So, let's discuss these three techniques and what they have to offer.

1. Universal Salary

For a good reason, a universal income is a popular method to remote salaries. It is based on a simple principle: if your job is location-independent, your income should be as well. Because they think that equal effort should be compensated equally, the Basecamp team pays their staff in this manner. This implies that when you establish compensation for your remote workers, regardless of whether they live in a high- or low-cost-of-living area, every job title is paid the same amount.

This, of course, has numerous advantages for you as a business. Setting a single wage saves you a lot of effort to work out the cost-of-living adjustments and track your employees' whereabouts. This means you'll be able to hire employees who live a nomadic lifestyle or constantly relocate without having to worry about updating their pay every time they do.

It's also one of the most equitable ways to compensate your staff because their location doesn't determine their income. Paying employees less purely because of their location can be demoralizing and unjust because salaries are typically perceived to symbolize how much a firm values an employee. When everyone in the same job role is paid the same, it reduces awkwardness among coworkers.

Universal compensation is also a smart way to increase your workforce's diversity. Given that people may not relocate, whether to another city or nation, you can still hire excellent talent regardless of where they originate.

The one big disadvantage of a universal income is that it can be unjust in some situations. If someone lives in a low-cost neighborhood but is paid the same as someone who lives in a more expensive area, two employees on the same wage may have drastically different living situations. It's also difficult for enterprises located in low-cost-of-living countries to set universal salaries competitive in high-cost-of-living countries. They may find it difficult to attract top-tier remote talent in these circumstances because such individuals can earn more money closer to home.

2. Cost of Living Salary

Employees are paid based on their location for a cost-of-living compensation, which is a contentious concept. That isn't to imply that it can't be effective in some situations.

To begin with, as previously said, a company headquartered in a low-cost-of-living area may have a difficult time attracting people from more expensive areas if salaries are established based on their local area. Adjusting for the cost of living also implies that you can save money on staff pay in less expensive places without sacrificing their quality of life. In most circumstances, this can help to balance the books by eliminating salary disparities due to location.

Adjusting pay, on the other hand, can have certain drawbacks in certain situations. Employees who reside in less expensive places may feel undervalued compared to those who live in more expensive nations or cities, leading to them being less engaged at work and harboring bad views toward their coworkers, managers, and your company as a whole. Are you going to reduce someone's wage because they relocate to a less expensive area? Because if that's the case, you can expect your employees to have a sour connection with you and your organization if you do it. This remote salary option also means that you'll have to devote a significant amount of time and resources to individually adjusting pay for the cost of living.

It's important to remember that it's not just a matter of changing your employees' salaries to account for their cost of living in a specific place, but also for their profession. Whether it's a town, city, or district, each has its labor market and conditions, with certain openings being simpler to fill than others. Utilize a simple cost of living adjustment calculator. You may find yourself offering much less than a local company because you haven't modified your wage offer to consider what else is available to candidates.

As a result, you'll need a system in place that takes the market data for each location into account and adjusts salaries accordingly. This can take a long time and a lot of effort to get right, especially if your organization has hundreds of employees. Another issue you face is keeping track of employee whereabouts and adjusting wages when they relocate.

3. Headquarter Salary

A headquarters salary, also known as a national average income, is based on the cost of living in your local area or the national average. Suppose your employees live in areas with a similar cost of living. In that case, this procedure makes it much easier to make modifications depending on it, and it also ensures that everyone is paid equally.

However, one drawback to this method is that your local area may limit your ability to hire distant workers. If your company is headquartered in London, this is less of an issue; however, if you have staff who live in a less costly city, such as Barcelona, you may find it difficult to recruit employees who live in a more expensive location, such as New York.

Have No Fear, Remote Work Is Here!

So, you're left with two possibilities. You can either try to discover talent in less costly places, which is a possibility, or you can make cost-of-living adjustments for people who live in more expensive areas. However, you're back to the same issue you'd have with a full cost of living pay.

If you've decided that working remotely is an option for you and want to give it a shot, you'll want to make your case as persuasively as possible. Don't pitch the concept to your boss over lunch. Your request is important, and it should be treated with care while adhering to all protocols. Request a face-to-face appointment with your boss for your request for the best results.

CHAPTER 5: MAKING THE SHIFT

How to Convince Your Boss to Let You Work Remotely

While remote work is becoming more popular, with demonstrated benefits for both businesses and individuals, a huge workforce segment is still unable to work remotely, even part-time. So, if you haven't already, how can you persuade your boss to let you work from home? I will tell you a few steps that worked for me.

1. Decide if it's really possible.

First, ask yourself the following questions: Is it possible for you to work from home in your current position? Is your job one where you could complete your work from home with no changes, inconveniences, or cost to your employer or clients? Could you work from home without jeopardizing your organization's security? If you can answer yes to these questions, you might be able to work from home.

If you're having problems answering these questions, make a list of the things you could perform remotely without requiring any adjustments from your employer, as well as the things you couldn't do without requiring any adjustments from your employer. After reviewing the list, you should swiftly assess whether or not remote work is a viable option for you. It's critical to be realistic about this first and most vital step.

It's worth noting that jobs in some highly regulated industries or require a high level of security may require you to work in an office setting. You might only be able to view documents and emails on-site.

2. Present Your Case Properly

manager to devote solely to your request. Also, don't be evasive about why you want to meet. Many business professionals will not schedule a meeting or return a phone call unless they know the discussion topic.

3. Make a Strategy

The worst thing you can do once your meeting has been scheduled is show up without a plan. You should arrive at the meeting with a well-thought-out strategy. You should anticipate the questions your boss will ask and be prepared to respond. Prepare an explanation of how the remote working arrangement will work and how it will benefit the company. So, before your meeting, be sure to have answers to the following questions:

- Do you want to work part-time or full-time from home?

- Would you be willing to give it a try? When will you begin, and for how long?

- What equipment or special access would you require to work from home or remotely, if any?
- What hours would you be available to work from home?
- When and how would your boss, employees, and clients be able to get in touch with you?

You could even write a formal proposal for your request, which your manager can evaluate and consider later, as your manager may not be able to respond to you immediately.

4. Assessing the advantages of the arrangement for your employer

You wouldn't seek your boss for permission to work from home if it didn't benefit you. You would benefit from not having to deal with traffic, distractions, or being away from home, to name a few. But how does your employer benefit from the arrangement.

When you originally applied for a job with your present employer, you had to persuade them that hiring you would improve their business. When it comes to remote work arrangements, the same logic applies. If you want to work from home, you'll need to persuade your boss why it's in the company's best interests for you to do so. The good news is that there is a wealth of material to assist you here. According to recent Stanford University research, productivity increased among employees allowed to work remotely and helped businesses save money.

Prepare a list of reasons why and how working remotely will help your employer based on your study and have it ready for your meeting.

5. Patience Is a Real Virtue

You may not have time to wait if your situation requires you to work remotely right away—for example, if your spouse is being moved to another area and you want to keep your job when you relocate. Otherwise, patience is the best course of action. It's possible that you won't gain approval to work remotely immediately or that you'll get a "yes, but" response. Perhaps remote work isn't typical in your industry or expertise. Perhaps it isn't common (yet) at your place of business.

If you don't obtain the response you want right away, kindly request that your manager remembers it for the future. Then come back to it in a few months.

Working from Home Rights

While several countries, such as the Netherlands, have already developed rules controlling working from home, the United States currently does not have such freedom. In other words, whether or not to allow flexible or home working is totally up to the company. There is no such thing as a home office law. Some employees with exceptional medical conditions or those closely caring for individuals with medical conditions may be entitled to apply to work from home under the Family Medical Leave Act (FMLA).

Have No Fear, Remote Work Is Here!

Employees who do not meet the FMLA's particular requirements are generally not permitted to work from home. The employer is the one who decides whether or not employees can work flexibly. Employees can make a relevant question if their company does not allow them to work from home. On the other hand, company owners are not legally obligated to comply and are free to reject applications for remote labor.

Employers usually tend to implement remote and flexible working for their employees as long as they keep accurate records of the hours worked, according to the US Fair Labor Standards Act. The relevant provisions can be added to an employee's employment contract if they are authorized to work from home. Additional flexible working conditions and frameworks can be agreed upon, such as how frequently an employee can work from home, how they can be contacted, what equipment is provided, and how overtime is computed. The requirements might be imposed as a supplement to an employee's existing employment contract if they did not already have the right to work from home.

An employment contract may not always have to include the opportunity to work from home. Labor agreements could potentially regulate flexible working arrangements. Within these laws, large firms with labor agreements can establish home office rights. Internally, management and a staff association or work council, if one exists, can specify home working provisions. The right to work from home, on the other hand, cannot be compelled and is always at the option of the employer.

Things to Consider for a Company Shifting Back to Office from Remote Work

Many employees may be concerned about reopening offices, but some will welcome the return to normality. In 2021, 27% of workers report finding it difficult to unplug while working from home, up from 9% in our first year working from home in 2020. This is reasonable; the distinction between our professional and personal life has become increasingly blurred. People are becoming anxious and seeking a small piece of normalcy, which for most means going back to work.

Here are four suggestions that would help if you belong to a company returning to the office after working remotely for a year or more.

1. Plan.

Anxiety can be reduced by planning. Going back to work doesn't feel so daunting if you have control over your working week and know what to expect. Even if you're not concerned about returning to work, planning can make the transition simpler.

Consider how you'll get to work. It may be tough to go to work, especially if you utilize public transportation and are wary of being so near to others. Consider driving for the first few months or booking a private ride through your ground transportation provider if you're seeking a more socially distant way to work. You might come to work feeling revitalized and ready to take on the day.

2. Have a conversation with your immediate supervisor.

Before you return to work, go to your line manager to determine what procedures are in place for social distancing and all employees' expectations. Some employers, for example, have requested that employees wipe down their workstations before leaving each day, wear masks when away from their computers, and eat lunch at their desks. Knowing what to expect can assist you in mentally preparing for the event.

If the idea of a 9-to-5 schedule makes you nervous, ask your boss if there's any way you could create a more flexible schedule. Maybe you'd rather work from the office for 2-3 days a week and from home the rest of the time. If travelling is a part of your job, you might profit from just one day in the office.

3. Review your travel policy.

If you travel for work, you'll need to be aware of your company's travel regulations in various regions. It's critical to understand how to access your travel policy and what is and isn't permitted, whether you're traveling locally or worldwide.

Your organization may have adopted a permissible travel framework due to COVID to keep travel to a bare minimum, which will assist you in defining what constitutes necessary travel. Your organization's procedures may change; for example, your organization's autonomy for reserving "safe" lodging may be removed.

If you're a travel manager, you'll need to factor in the possibility of employee quarantine upon their return to the country if they travel internationally. The red-listed countries change regularly, as we all know, due to localized outbreaks.

4. Be considerate of others.

If you're a manager, you're well aware that each employee is unique. We all have various concerns, and anxiousness is understandable in instances like this. That's why it's critical to be patient and accepting of your coworkers - not everyone will be delighted to be back at work.

It's a great idea to reach out to coworkers before returning to the office, especially those you feel comfortable being open to. Creating a support network at work can make a move back to work go more smoothly.

Misconceptions About Remote Work

According to the 2019 Global State of Remote Work report, 68 percent of global workers have worked remotely, and the number is growing. Despite this, there are still misconceptions and stigmas concerning remote employment, such as work clothing (do remote employees ever dress?) and degree of dedication (if they can't be bothered to come to an office, they can't possibly care that much).

It's time to say goodbye to stereotypes. Here are a few fallacies about remote work that the skeptics have debunked.

1. Remote employees are less productive.

One of the greatest fears among business owners considering hiring remote workers is that team members will be less effective without on-site supervision and management. There are various ways to manage remote workers and measure productivity in today's world of time tracking apps, chat boards, and websites like Slack. "Holding employees accountable by building a flexible procedure and employing tools to follow the process" is the key.

In fact, companies who employ this method discover that remote team members are more productive than office workers. The bigger issue is overwork and burnout, which is exacerbated by the temptation to work longer hours without the regular support of coworkers and managers.

2. Remote workers are less qualified.

Another myth is that most skilled professionals prefer to work in a formal office setting, while remote workers are individuals who just do not meet the qualifications for management jobs. This fallacy is especially widespread when a worker is a freelancer or independent contractor who is thought to be less capable of expanding their abilities. Most of the leaders prefer the independence and autonomy of self-employment, and many have established a high degree of expertise and motivation over their careers.

Hiring remote workers gives you access to some of the most talented people in any field. Geographical boundaries no longer restrict companies, and they can broaden their employment pool to include people from other states, regions, and even countries. This broadens the search for the absolute finest in the field. "The only way to obtain the best people is to recruit talent without regard to geography.

3. Finding Remote Workers Is Difficult

How to discover and recruit workers is a fundamental concern that arises for a company considering the usage of remote teams. They could be former workers or contractors in some circumstances, but finding elite personnel will almost always involve a concerted networking effort. LinkedIn, for example, allows you to start building a pool of possible hires from its over 200 million users. Some websites feature a variety of project-based contractors and freelancers that might be interested in a longer-term commitment.

International freelancer networking networks for specialized industries, such as software development and engineering, are also available to businesses. Participating on these sites can lead to meetings with established contractors in a certain region or country.

4. Communicating and managing remote workers is difficult.

Communication and management across various distances and time zones without losing connection and inclusion are natural issues for a remote workforce. "How can I know what my team member is doing and what progress is being made?" is the main concern for an employer. Although not every remote worker is adept at self-management, there are apps and solutions available to help them overcome this potential issue.

Online checklist boards like Trello or Basecamp, which allow team members to communicate, upload work products, and signal project progress, are one approach to define and monitor milestones. Slack is a messaging program for remote teams with real-time message boards similar to Skype but can link many teams and create the illusion of a virtual workplace. These solutions can help remote teams overcome communication and management issues, allowing them to focus on actual performance and project success.

5. IT and data entry are the only jobs that can be done remotely.

For certain technical work, customer support, and data entry professions, remote workers have long been accepted. Businesses know that projects can be outsourced or contracted hourly on an individual basis because these positions do not require a physical location or direct supervision.

On the other hand, remote work teams do not have to be restricted to specific categories, and online collaboration and communication tools enable the formation of a "virtual office" for various corporate operations. While IT development jobs are still in high demand, teams can also be assembled for sales and marketing, product development, creative work, and customer service.

Consider Your Personality Type Before Going into Remote Work

Working from home isn't without its drawbacks. Adjustments must be made, and they must be much more basic than simply remembering to clean up the background on Skype or Zoom. Many people have noticed a relationship between lockdown and introversion on social media. "I've been practicing #socialdistancing for much of my life," as numerous tweets put it. Even Introverts, however, will not enjoy working from home if the conditions aren't right, especially when, as in the current crisis, remote working has been imposed suddenly, causing concerns about friends and family, a loss of face-to-face social contact, the closure of pubs, cinemas, and restaurants, and no sense of clarity about how long this will all last.

HR specialists and managers must now consider how employees with various attitudes and personality preferences will react and bear the stress, uncertainty, and new reality of working from home.

As employed by the Myers-Briggs Type Indicator® (MBTI®) assessment, the type method is one of the most prominent ways of characterizing personality. This test examines four aspects of personality: whether we prefer to focus our attention on the outside world (Extraversion, E) or our inner world of thoughts and feelings (Introversion, I); whether we want to deal with detailed, concrete information (Sensing, S) or the big picture (Intuition, N); and whether we prefer to make decisions based on objective logic (Thinking, T) or the basis of intuition (Intuition, N) (Perceiving, P).

The MBTI model has the benefit of being simple enough for people to rapidly understand something about their personality and the personality of others in situations like the current crisis. People who know and understand their MBTI type can use the framework, with the support of HR and L&D professionals, to help them adapt to virtual working. The E-I and J-P parts of the MBTI type are particularly important.

Personality Types that are and aren't Geared for Remote Work

1. **ISTJ: Responsible Realists**

This personality type is extremely organized, which is a huge plus in a remote working situation. They are responsible doers who value clarity, enjoy routines, and value honor, hard effort, and social duty. They're reserved, quiet, and dependable. They don't require much supervision or monitoring; simply email them a to-do list at the start of the week, and you can trust them to get on with it silently. They'd also be ideal for organizing and streamlining any shared online environment, from Dropbox to Google Docs.

2. INFJ: Insightful Visionaries

The entire hiring process is far more challenging in a virtual environment, but INFJ(s) can be an ace up your sleeve. They tend to be outstanding judges of character, so having them sit in on virtual interviews would be a tremendous asset. If you can, avoid putting them front and center in any Zoom meetings. They don't thrive on attention and prefer to work in the background. They are conscientious creatives who are quietly assertive but also intuitive about people and care about the feelings of their coworkers. They are usually deep thinkers with a plethora of ideas.

3. INTJ: Conceptual Planners

They are meticulous innovators who are at ease working alone and flourish in a virtual office setting. This personality type is a natural problem solver who excels at taking a concept and turning it into a strategy. They may think intuitively as well as practically. This group is more likely to communicate via text, so they'll need to be persuaded to pick up the phone or join a Zoom session when it's more convenient. They're deadline-driven, but there's a risk they'll make rash decisions, especially if they don't have colleagues to check their inclinations. INTJs need to be reminded to take a breather, take their time, and let ideas develop rather than rushing right into them.

4. ISFJ: Practical Helpers

They are as follows: ISFJs prioritize peace and cooperation, have a strong work ethic, and are sensitive to colleagues' needs and feelings, making them the most extroverted of the introverts. Their zeal, however, is tempered by the fact that they are usually incredibly conscientious employees who are natural managers, capable of keeping distant teams united and happy. ISFJs have a keen eye for detail, which makes them ideal for double-checking others' work, editing shared papers, and finalizing pitches and proposals. They're also great at following rules and inspiring others to do the same, so put them in charge of any time tracking software you're using and watch them boost your entire team's productivity.

5. ISTP: Logical Pragmatists

They are straightforward, to-the-point personalities who are devoted to their peers yet unconcerned with laws and norms. Because they are normally reasonable and logical but may also be exuberant and spontaneous, ISTPs are the most unpredictable of the 16 personality types. Virtuosos will most certainly feel the impact of missed day-to-day encounters with their teams, so periodic one-on-one digital meetings will help them maintain motivation and attention. Because ISTPs excel at debugging, they can be a valuable tech asset in a remote work environment. They're great at trying out new tools and navigating software, but they're also prone to losing concentration. They're the team member who's most likely to switch off their camera at a meeting, open a new window, and start surfing the web; thus, they must be managed.

6. ISFP: Versatile Supporters

They are sensitive creators who thrive when they can help others. They are affable, approachable, and avoid confrontation. They also recognize the importance of trying new things and having fresh experiences. This group enjoys living in the now and can easily become absorbed in their task. They need to be reminded to take an hour for lunch and complete the working day at a decent time when working from home and without coworkers physically supervising them. Their energy is a valuable resource, but it must occasionally be harnessed and guided in the proper direction by others.

7. INFP: Thoughtful Idealists

INFPs can get lost in their ideas and daydreams since they are laid-back idea people with a well-developed value system. While they contribute vigor and zeal to initiatives, they typically struggle to maintain their enthusiasm for long periods of time. This personality type has deeply held ideals, which can lead to issues when they are offended. When working remotely, this is accentuated because grievances can linger longer; therefore, managers must encourage employees to air their grievances. Otherwise, encouraging and reinforcing purpose in their work is the key to getting the most out of this group. In other words, if their efforts reflect their ideals, this group has the potential to be unstoppable.

8. INTP: Objective Analysts

They are outlaw problem solvers who appreciate patterns, are quick to see inconsistencies, and value expertise and rationality. They want to be alone and will prefer lockdown over any other type. This personality needs to be allowed the freedom to do things their own way and to be heard because they are the ones that come up with the best answers. Their flaw is that they frequently fail to share decisions and solutions, a feature that is exacerbated when working from home. Encourage anyone who is an INTP on your team to use shared documents and tools as much as feasible.

9. ESTP: Energetic Problem Solvers

They are high-risk takers who thrive on solving large challenges quickly. They are dedicated to their goals, but they can become impatient with longer-term initiatives due to their short attention spans. They can be a valuable asset to any team, but they can also be difficult to manage due to their disdain for regulations. To work with them, you must keep things lighthearted and going quickly. This personality type is known for being impatient, so instead of setting long-term goals, offer them a day's worth of chores in a project tool. They excel at thinking outside the box, so don't confine them to one by suffocating their imagination.

10. ESFP: Enthusiastic Improvisers

This personality type wants to show up and show off, and they are the life and soul of the office. They're vivacious, enthusiastic, and natural performers who frequently pursue careers in the arts or creative fields. They enjoy being in the spotlight, but they're also compassionate, friendly, and generous people. Remote working can tire them because they need time to shine in front of people. Get them involved in films, voiceovers, podcasts, or any other activity that requires creative performance as often as possible. They'll also be fantastic in remote pitches, as they'll add a convincing intensity that a computer screen might lack.

11. ENFP: Imaginative Motivators

They are perceptive people-pleasers who enjoy experimenting and discovering new things. They have a strong, intuitive temperament and enjoy being in the company of others, relying on emotions rather than reasoning. Importantly, they are motivated more by personal ambitions than by financial gain. This group excels at both idea-generating and collaborative tasks, so they'd be a valuable addition to any brainstorming sessions or big-picture thinking. Their flaw is that they aren't the best starters or finishers; thus, meeting deadlines can be difficult. When working remotely, this can be worsened because they don't always get communications or respond to colleagues quickly enough. As a result, to realize their high creative worth, they frequently require gentle management.

12. ENTP: Enterprising Explorers

They're charismatic geniuses with a penchant for tying knots. This category includes several CEOs. This personality type is objective, logical, and sensible, but it requires regular mental stimulation. For the most part, leaders and managers like to concentrate on big concepts and avoid monotonous duties and procedures. Play to their strengths: they are excellent debaters. This group excels at developing new goods and ideas and larger conversations about how to drive the company forward. They're also great at dazzling clients and proposing new business, so bring them along on any pivotal Zoom conversations. You might only have to remind them to silence themselves now and then since if they don't, they'll take over the chat.

13. ESTJ: Efficient Organizers

They are traditional, organized, hardworking, systematic, and devoted decision-makers who are pragmatic. They'd be the veteran captain of your company's sports team. This group enjoys organizing themselves, others, and the world around them, which can be a positive trait but can also come across as domineering and confrontational, especially when giving orders without making eye contact. They frequently need to be reminded to be courteous with others, especially in a workplace where they communicate largely via email or messaging apps, leaving their statements open to interpretation.

14. ESFJ: Supportive Contributors

They are nurturing caregivers who thrive when they can help others. This group is gregarious, polite, and courteous, and they prioritize the needs of others. They'll be the ones that send direct messages to colleagues to inquire about their well-being, all while attempting to organize online quizzes and virtual happy hours. Because people enjoy working for them, this personality type makes the ideal project manager. They're both organized and thoughtful, making them excellent for completing jobs on time. They'd also be a good candidate for remote onboarding new hires because of their kind, patient demeanor.

15. ENFJ: Compassionate Facilitators

They are also natural leaders, but they are guided by intuition and feelings rather than logic and reason, unlike their ENTP counterparts. If they're in charge, they're the inspirational type: highly motivated and sensitive to the needs of people around them. This set of diplomats is known for putting others' needs ahead of their own, which can be problematic in terms of burnout and accomplishing their own obligations. However, the positives far outnumber the negatives in this group. Even if they aren't in a leadership capacity, having Protagonists lead group conversations is usually a smart idea because they excel at it. They should be your go-to Zoom meeting host, and they should be at the center of every circumstance that involves discussion, consensus, or bringing people and ideas together.

16. ENTJ: Decisive Strategists

They are logical problem solvers who enjoy breaking down barriers and finding answers. They place a high priority on knowledge and have limited tolerance for inefficiency. They are mostly concerned with goal-setting, structure, and organization. They are personable and self-assured, and they can inspire others to work toward a common objective. This personality type is drawn to huge visions and major decisions, which can be problematic when working from home. When implementing plans, they don't always perceive the finer details, and in a remote working environment, this puts them at danger of making decisions without adequately considering the perspectives of others. ENTJs must remember to strike a balance between directing and consulting to genuinely excel.

Introversion vs. Extraversion (I-E)

Extraverts appreciate a busy, energetic setting with lots of opportunities for interaction. When working from home, this may not be easy to achieve, especially because the options for social interaction outside of work are greatly decreased. Extraverts should take regular breaks and make their environment more stimulating, such as listening to music or walking away from their desk for a brief period of time. This may be merely within their home or flat, or it could be outside; after all, official recommendations suggest that we exercise outdoors at least once a day.

Extraverts should make use of this, but not as an excuse to over socialize. Businesses should use online platforms like Zoom or Skype to communicate and organize regular informal meetings and virtual get-togethers. Extraverts may need to organize periods that are free of distractions if they need to do focused work without the formal procedures of the office.

Many Introverts have been forced to act in a more "extraverted" manner until lately, and some will welcome the peace and quiet of the "new normal." They want a tranquil, peaceful setting and may prefer to work from home if there aren't many other people, particularly youngsters, in the vicinity. They do, however, require some interaction with the outside world, and they must engage and communicate with family, friends, and coworkers to prevent being isolated. Others should remember to include them; some Introverts risk becoming so absorbed in their profession or interest that they forget everything else. Regular breaks are beneficial to Introverts as well.

Judging and Perceiving (J-P)

People with a Judging preference love a planned, structured life; thus, the imposed shift of working from home and the disturbance to their routine that this caused may have been quite upsetting to them. It will be beneficial for individuals to get into a new habit as quickly as possible, and it will be critical for companies to make this possible.

This will be especially important when employees have been furloughed, settled into a new routine, and then returned to work. Setting clear professional and personal goals at the outset of each day and establishing working hours, and making time for other activities, such as shopping, to take longer than usual, will be beneficial. Organizations that have asked employees to work fewer hours should be extremely clear about what this involves.

Remote work has both benefits and disadvantages for the Perceiving preference. Many aspects of working from home may appeal to someone with this inclination, including the ability to be flexible with hours, especially when the sun is shining (if they have a garden). On the other hand, Restrictions may make it difficult to be spontaneous, and working from home can lead to a routine that they may find demotivating. Keeping them fresh requires diversity, which can be achieved by switching between different activities or work assignments. Informal virtual meetings and get-togethers with a 'jovial' tone might also be beneficial.

Bringing it all together as a whole type

Have No Fear, Remote Work Is Here!

The other components of the MBTI model, Sensing-Intuition (S-N) and Thinking-Feeling (T-F), also play a role in determining how stressful the current situation will be for people and how they will react to it. Without the typical signs of face-to-face interaction, thinking folks' online communication can be very clear and task-focused, with curt, impersonal emails or IMs, leaving those with a Feeling preference wondering what they did wrong. Being mindful of the needs of others will help both of you feel less stressed.

CHAPTER 6: SOCIAL MEDIA REVOLUTION

How do hiring managers hire employees through social media?

Social media has evolved as a popular recruitment channel for attracting top-tier prospects, thanks to extraordinary innovations that are constantly redefining the talent acquisition environment. In reality, in today's hot candidate-driven labor market, finding great personnel can be incredibly difficult for human resources professionals who do not abandon traditional hiring tactics. It's because the competition for top talent is becoming increasingly strong, and organizations all around the world are experiencing a severe talent shortage. This is why most HR managers work hard to incorporate social recruiting into their hiring strategy. Businesses that want to speed up their hiring process can use social media recruiting to find potential job prospects, making it easier to build a high-quality talent pool in less time. Some of the most effective social media hiring tactics used by hiring managers to find qualified candidates are listed below.

Have No Fear, Remote Work Is Here!

1. *Increasing the company's web presence.*

Create a strong brand and become the firm that everyone wants to work with. Make yourself the expert in your subject. Don't just focus on customers when it comes to branding. They might be the folks you need to help your company grow from the inside if they've already invested in you.

Give millennials something to be enthusiastic about if you want them to form an emotional connection with your organization. Organically attract prospects by sharing information that portrays your firm positively and demonstrates that it is a fantastic place to work.

Consider the frequently mentioned firms, the ones with distinctive working cultures and excellent employee perks - how can you join them?

Above everything, maintain consistency. Have a unified voice, stay on message, and be transparent about your principles, ethics, and convictions.

2. *Using video to entice passive applicants to participate.*

If you want to take your relationship to the next level, you must engage with them once you've established your presence on your preferred social media sites.

And video is one of the most powerful means of engagement. Users on social media are 10 times more likely to engage with video than any other type of material. According to 52 percent of marketing professionals worldwide, it's the type of content that delivers the best return on investment. Use video's attraction to attract passive applicants and other industry professionals.

3. Encourage staff to share social media posts.

The goal of social media is to broaden your audience. Make use of your current staff network to spread the word. Encourage your staff to participate in the recruitment drive by asking them to share your messages on social media. Whether from those trying to hire or those looking to be hired, the value of a personal recommendation should never be underestimated. Furthermore, social media sharing is one of the most effective ways to find new employees. Simply make sure your company has a social media policy in place and that all staff know what is expected of them. After all, they will be your brand ambassadors, and you don't want them to harm your business's reputation by accident.

4. Participate in LinkedIn groups.

Recruiters use LinkedIn to find talent in an estimated 87 percent of cases (55 percent use Facebook and 47 percent use Twitter). Join and engage in LinkedIn groups relevant to your sector, in addition to optimizing your company's LinkedIn page to demonstrate you're actively recruiting (which you should clearly do).

On LinkedIn, there are many specialized forums where applicants are actively involved, attempting to establish themselves in their area and actively seek them out. You can join The Sales Association group for sales and business development professionals, for example, if you're employing salespeople.

It's all about the power of networking, and you can readily uncover top talent and important influencers in these organizations. When it comes to attracting the proper specialists, knowing who these folks are will make your life a lot easier.

5. Using other social media channels, such as Reddit.

It's also worth noting that different techniques should be tried based on every social media network you're using: one size does not fit all, and what works for Twitter may not necessarily work for LinkedIn or Facebook. Take advantage of the fact that all of these social networks were created to appeal to different audiences, be utilized in different ways, and use that to your advantage. Determine which profile receives the most engagement and stick with it. Create profiles on Reddit, Snapchat, Instagram, and YouTube, as well as the big three (Facebook, Linked In, and Twitter).

6. Providing high-quality information.

Whether it's your own or curated, if you're distributing content, make sure it doesn't come off as spam. Recognize the questions that your audience is posing and provide answers to them. Maintain their interest. If you don't have anything that others want to share, social media won't work for you –

and that's kind of the point of being social in the first place. It is necessary for your material to be amusing, useful, or fascinating.

It doesn't matter what format you use:

- videos.
- how-to manuals.
- Podcasts.
- Blog.
- Articles.
- Pictures.
- Infographics.

Basically, everything that isn't a simple truth or the length of a boring sentence. Give them something worth sharing if you want your work to become viral.

7. Using data to improve the social media advertising plan.

Because you can target who sees your ad on social media, it works extremely effectively. Unlike traditional advertising, when you're playing a numbers game and hoping to find your gem in the muck among the millions of individuals who saw the ad, social media advertising focuses on your ideal candidates since you select your search parameters. However, suppose you actually want to boost the effectiveness of your social media recruiting strategy. In that case, you need to use the data-gathering tools at your disposal to fine-tune your advertising campaign, so make sure to include measurable KPIs while creating your ad.

8. Maintaining potential recruits' interest – create a community

Instead of bombarding your audience with poor material, as previously stated, give them something to engage with and create a community of like-minded individuals.

Instead of bombarding them with information and creating a one-way street, start a discussion and carry it on. Send direct messages to people in your network who might be interested in joining your talent cloud. Discuss the company with them, as well as the advantages and possibilities of working there. Don't wait for your audience to come to you; be proactive and go to them.

9. Make use of the hashtag.

Take the time to learn about the power of the hashtag. It's all too easy to slap a # in front of a word or a sentence and expect it to perform its magic - but it's not that easy. Know your hashtags' reach, how many people use them, where they're used, and who they're used by — if your hashtag isn't addressing your target audience, it's pointless, so get rid of it.

On the other hand, if it becomes too popular, your message may get lost in the tidal wave of other messages that are also using it. Try to be creative with your hashtags, and tailor them to you, your organization, and the goals you want to achieve.

How to avoid getting distracted by social media while working remotely

Working from home necessitates maintaining concentration on the task at hand despite potential distractions and interruptions. Being hijacked into compulsive scrolling through social media feeds is one of the biggest temptations for both employers and employees.

More individuals are working from home these days, which means more time is spent on digital distractions like social media. And, given the large number of people who have joined the remote-working ranks due to the coronavirus, avoiding the temptation to spend too much time on social media has become much more difficult.

3 Ways to Keep Your Social Media Use Under Control While Working from Home

A global epidemic adds to regular updates, and many people seek news and check-in with friends and family on social media throughout the day.

While this can help you feel more connected to individuals you know but can't see during quarantines, being too focused on continually checking and refreshing can make it difficult to get work done from home. Too much time spent on social media, regardless of the circumstances, can have a negative impact on your attitude and productivity.

Here are some suggestions that helped me manage and regulate my social media use and work more efficiently from home by being focused, productive, and on schedule!

1. *Keep an eye on your usage.*

If you were already a heavy social media user, you might have noticed that the amount of time you spend reading through your feeds has increased since COVID-19 was placed on the global radar screen. But if you're not sure whether or how much this is harming your productivity, there's an easy method to find out: keep note of how you use different platforms.

Of course, there's an app for that—many of them, in fact—but you can also keep a simple time diary for a week or two to get a sense of how much time you spend on sites like Facebook, Instagram, or Twitter. Count how many minutes or hours you spend on social media each day, as well as on your work projects and other responsibilities.

Also, keep track of how long you spend doing each task so you can determine if there are any times of day when your focus and concentration are particularly difficult. Then, at the end of the week, go over your log to see if your social media usage has gotten out of hand. If it is, continue to the instructions below.

2. Learn to Control Your Checking Times

Because of the addictive nature of social feeds, it's difficult to trust yourself to control how much time you spend on them. Setting aside time for social media-free work hours, as well as blocks of time (such as lunch) to check your feeds, can help you overcome your problem.

When making this plan, start with your meetings and job tasks as your "big rocks" or top priorities. Block off time on your calendar to devote to dedicated project work, and then fill in the gaps with shorter blocks as needed. You'll love social media more and be more productive if you see it as a prize for a job well done rather than allowing it to consume your entire day.

3. Think about taking a social media detox or hiatus.

If you've done the first two steps and still feel like you've been scrolling through your social media feeds all day, you may need to take a bigger step to break the cycle. Taking a deliberate break from your "checking" behavior will help you get back to a more focused place where you can finish your task without being distracted by wanting to see what others are up to.

Your digital detox can last as little as a day if you avoid social media or as long as you're willing and able to limit your information intake. If you can take a break from picking up your phone and scrolling through social media to see what's new, you'll have more time to think about—and complete—other assignments.

Take a Break

With everything going on, the constant barrage of information can add to the stress of an already stressful and emotional scenario. Taking a break from monitoring social media updates regularly can help you be more focused and effective while working from home and relax your mind so you can focus on what really matters.

The role of social media in Remote Working

To a large extent, social media may be beneficial to distant employees.

1. Employees are able to take a mental break.

Taking a mental vacation from work sometimes is not something to be discouraged. Many firms already encourage employees to take short, regular breaks while on the job. Allowing employees to access social media during these breaks makes them more convenient. They wouldn't waste their time meandering through their home office on multiple devices. However, when utilized correctly, social media may provide your employees with the mental breaks they require throughout the day.

2. Enables employees to form and maintain professional relationships.

Your staff can improve professional contacts with people outside the organization by using social media platforms. These connections can then lead to opportunities that would not have been available otherwise. Sales leads, interest in employment, business prospects, and new ideas may arise from more and better relationships. LinkedIn is designed expressly for these kinds of interactions and has a slew of obvious business applications.

3. Employees can ask inquiries and address problems at work.

Employees can use social media to assist them in dealing with a bad work situation. If an employee is having trouble solving a problem, social media may be the solution. Posing a question on social media is a quick and easy approach to receive multiple answers. Even if none of the answers are used to address the problem, the information they provide may inspire a different approach. When you need a fresh perspective, social networking is a great way to get several new perspectives fast, conveniently, and free.

4. Develops and strengthens personal relationships with coworkers.

Coworkers can utilize social media to communicate with one another and strengthen their bonds. Employee relationships that are stronger result in more cohesive and productive work teams. Social media is a simple approach to encourage employees to communicate with one another, share ideas, and enhance engagement at work and home. Because social media can be accessed practically anywhere, your employees can communicate with one another even when they are not at work. Employee morale and engagement will be boosted by chance to communicate outside of work. Your work teams, in particular, may improve as they become closer.

5. *Improves the finding and transmission of information*

Employees can utilize social media as a medium of communication to discover and deliver job-related information, similar to number three on our list. Workers might use social media in the workplace to locate information relevant to their jobs or learn new skills that they can utilize while on the job. It's also a means for your staff to spread the word about your business. This information dissemination can help raise brand awareness and provide new prospects for recruiting and business.

6.*Enhances staff retention and recognition*

Internally and externally, social media is a fantastic tool for acknowledging staff achievements. Your firm can use social media to recognize exceptional performance, work anniversaries, new recruits, and other events. This acknowledgment encourages team members to connect, which helps to strengthen team bonds. Employees can congratulate one another, stay up to date on corporate news, and communicate with more of their coworkers. Social media may boost employee morale by providing opportunities for interaction and recognition. Employees who are more invested in their company and their coworkers are more inclined to stay.

7. Increases the productivity of the organization

Contrary to popular assumptions, using social media in the workplace may not negatively influence productivity. In fact, social media may be able to help your employees achieve levels of productivity they have yet to achieve.

According to a McKinsey Global Institute survey, while 72 percent of organizations use social media, the majority do not use it to its full potential. According to this study, businesses that fully embrace social media use (including an internal social media site) can increase employee productivity by 20 to 25%. Every company wishes for its workers to be more productive. Social media is a low-cost, easy-to-implement strategy that can boost your company's efficiency.

CHAPTER 7: REMOTE COMMUNICATION

How to Lay Off a Remote Worker

Regardless of how hard you try as a leader, there will come a time when you must split from an employee. The majority of HR experts recommend In-person terminations. In-person terminations are not always possible, especially as the number of remote and worldwide employees grows. The cost of having an employee come into the office or having a representative travel to the employee's place of employment for a termination meeting must be factored in. Travel coordination is often an issue when immediate action is required. Many businesses are being compelled to consider other options for communicating terminations.

Video conferencing or phone terminations are the next best options. When addressing sensitive matters like work status, videoconferencing allows all parties to see and understand nonverbal gestures, which is critical. Employers can communicate essential information and empathy to employees via videoconferencing or phone terminations, while employees can ask questions and share their perspectives.

While employee terminations are inconvenient for everyone, the following guiding principles helped me the most in navigating separation with remote employees as effectively and courteously as feasible.

1. Be ready.

Ensure to have a copy of your separation agreement with you when you start the meeting so you may refer to it. It's also crucial to prepare any correspondence you'll need to deliver the news that the employee is no longer with the organization and how anyone who wishes them well can contact them.

2. Plan ahead of time for off boarding requirements.

The majority of remote employees have access and permissions to your shared software and server that allows them to complete their tasks. Before the separation meeting, make sure you remove any sensitive tools or IT access for the employee.

Depending on the circumstances, it may be conceivable to keep the employee linked and active on the team-communication software to pass over responsibilities, files, and other information before leaving.

3. Use video conferencing to improve empathy and communication.

Video calls are a great method to ensure that you're leading with empathy and humanity as your workforce becomes more distributed, especially during the most difficult conversations.

Because you're both on camera, you can read and understand each other's body language, facial expressions, and general tone. It's also a good idea to assess reactions so you can figure out if there's a disconnect.

4. Get started as soon as possible.

Try to plan the termination call earlier in the day; working a full shift just to get "that call" at the end of the day is never a good sensation. It's best to ask to jump on a call first thing in the morning rather than later in the day to minimize undue anxiety.

5. Inform the team.

Every employee is a part of your team and culture, and they are inextricably linked to at least some of their coworkers. When people are separated, it's natural for them to experience a range of feelings and reactions. Make an effort to set the tone and get ahead of the topic.

Another facet of open communication is this. It's critical to share the essential information with other staff. Maintain a positive tone in your communications to keep morale up and reassure other employees that their jobs are secure.

Using e-mail to send news of a job separation is the least ideal method for a remote termination. E-mail, unlike video conferencing or the phone, does not allow for a real-time, two-way dialogue; it is impersonal, leaving an employee feeling disrespected or inconsequential, and may trigger a negative emotional reaction in the terminated employee. Furthermore, there are dangers associated with email termination, such as delaying the receipt of the termination notice, mistakenly deleting the notice, sending information to the incorrect email address, and failing to include vital information or attachments. When communicating a change in job status, employers should use email as a last resort.

How to Manage Your Inbox While Working Remotely

More than 269 billion emails are sent every day (that's 149,513 emails every minute), and it can feel like they all land up in our mailbox. Given that more people are working remotely and relying more on electronic messages, volume is expected to rise. It's all too easy to devote a significant amount of your working day to clear your email inbox at the expense of other, often more essential, concerns.

I despise emails with all of my heart. They're a hassle to write, even more so to read, and at a time when most internal communication takes place through messaging apps, they seem obnoxious. But, like it or not, emails aren't going away anytime soon. Indeed, I'm sure we're all seeing an increase in our inboxes due to the coronavirus outbreak. Because, let's face it, you're probably settling into work from home until further notice; I'll give some tips to assist you in handling your inbound emails.

Take command.

The most aggravating aspect of emails is that you have no control over how many you receive per day or who sends them to you. As I type this, I can see that I have over 70 emails in my Inbox, none of which were sent by me.

If you work for a firm that uses internal communication technologies like Slack and your job doesn't require you to send or receive emails, you're in a unique situation since you can afford to ignore your inbox. This may appear frightening, but it does not have to be. It's all about finding the right balance!

Strike the right chord.

Consider the following scenario: You're working on a report. When you receive an email notice, you put down what you're doing and quickly click to read it. You must respond to this email and send a few internal emails to check on the status of a project. Following your colleagues' responses, you must check many assets before sending them to your customer. By the time you've finished, you're likely to have completely forgotten what you were doing before and, worse, lost your line of thought.

There's no denying that email is distracting. I will recommend you set a time limit for reading and responding. To do this properly, consider how you operate and what needs your attention at times. Make a schedule for yourself and select when you want to respond to inbound queries. For instance, you could make it a habit to check your emails first thing in the morning and an hour before you log out for the day. If you don't have any situations that require your urgent attention, sticking to this timetable should be simple for you.

Making things work in your favor

The beauty of technology is that you don't have to accomplish this by yourself. There are numerous tools available to assist you in making emails work for you. Adiós, for example, is a free solution for Gmail (and other Google-based inboxes) that allows you to hide incoming emails until specific times based on your needs. It really suggests that you choose three distinct time slots each day, but you may also configure your incoming emails to appear every hour.

You can add senders whose messages you need to read as soon as they arrive, and emails sent from non-registered addresses can be checked using the "Deliver emails immediately" button if you need to keep a watch on emails from a specific individual.

Maintain a strict routine.

Another amazing Gmail-based application is Boomerang. It allows you to draught an email and schedule it to be sent at a later time - it's all about having emails work for you rather than slaving away in your inbox. It's quite simple to use. Simply type your messages as usual, then click the 'Send later option. You can also set a reminder if no one responds or to assist you in overcoming your anxiety of not replying.

Mindfulness

I've been using Mailtrack for several years and can't say enough good things about it. To track when your email is opened, you may download the Chrome extension for free and plug it into your Gmail-based email account. Most users will be happy with the free version, which includes limitless email tracking. Still, if you want more information, such as full email metrics or daily reports, you should consider upgrading to a premium subscription. Knowing that your email has been read gives you peace of mind and allows you to move on to other things without constantly checking to see if someone has responded.

This isn't a full list, but I believe it will assist you in reducing email anxiety and increasing your productivity.

How to Clarify Email Communication when Working Remotely

An email is a crucial tool for collaboration, communication, and other tasks as remote work becomes more common in today's employment market.

However, because consumers get many emails daily, it might not be easy to create effective emails. With so many emails in one's inbox, there's a risk that someone will see your sent email in seconds. As a result, consumers must be able to open and read your email without having to hunt through their inbox to discover it. Although you have no control over how or when people react to emails, these seven methods can help individuals deliver you what you need more quickly.

1. Come up with a subject that grabs your attention.

You must first capture your recipients' attention in order for them to open and read your email. You'll be able to attract readers' attention when they're deciding which emails to open first by developing an engaging email topic. Normally, people prioritize which emails to open based on their importance. As a result, if your subject line isn't interesting enough, people won't open your email.

2. Make use of the BLUF formula

The acronym BLUF stands for "Bottom Line Up Front." In other words, revealing what you want at the end isn't a smart idea – you're not creating a mystery novel with a ludicrous plot twist at the conclusion. Many remote professionals make the mistake of offering justification before making a request. That is not how a professional email should be written. Instead, present the request first, followed by supporting arguments, so that the receiver can comprehend the reasoning in the context of the request and is more likely to respond by email.

3. When sending requests, be specific and set a deadline.

It's critical to be explicit about what you're looking for and who you're asking to do the work when asking recipients for something. You should never assume or think that someone else is doing the work for you. Also, don't be afraid to give receivers a deadline when asking for anything, especially if the deadline is important. Also, if necessary, call recipients to follow up if they have a habit of checking their email several times a day.

Also, bear the following in mind while setting a deadline:

- Prepare ahead of time.

- Set a firm deadline (one that works for both the sender and the recipient).

- Never impose deadlines on the spur of the moment. (In other words, don't schedule a deadline for a short period of time).

Giving receivers a fair deadline increases the likelihood of the task being completed rather than being disregarded or rushed. People nowadays work from home while juggling other responsibilities, allowing them to be more flexible. Never, ever take advantage of other people's efforts to balance work and life.

4. Email and Instant Messaging Are Not the Same

Email isn't a substitute for instant messaging. In reality, people are more likely to respond to instant messengers (including chat, texting, and other forms of communication) while they are on their mobile devices. People can read emails on their cellphones and tablets, or they can wait until the recipient gets home to read them on a desktop computer or laptop. Make a phone call or use an instant messaging app if your communication is urgent. Consider the three-email rule while sending emails: Make a phone call if anything hasn't been resolved after three email exchanges.

5. Make an emailing schedule

Email scheduling is a fantastic technique to keep emails from becoming casual instant messaging. And, while you're contacting your boss or coworkers, scheduling allows you to keep your emotions in check. Email scheduling allows you to properly juggle work and life without sacrificing one or the other.

6. Use A Canned Out-Of-Office Response When Away

You should take a break from your computer now and then. As a result, setting up a scripted out-of-office answer informs them that you'll be away and will read incoming emails when you get back to your computer.

Keep the following goals in mind while you create a scripted response:

- When you return, will you be able to make that commitment to rely on?

- Do you want other people's emails to be sent to you again when you return?

Have No Fear, Remote Work Is Here!

- Do you want them to contact you right away if there's an emergency?

- Are there any compelling reasons for you to work irregular hours? (For example, daycare).

7. Make Use of Add-Ons to Improve Clarity and Writing

Users nowadays will utilize a variety of add-ons to ensure that their documents are error-free and understandable. As a result, it's not surprising that most people will use these add-ons while sending business emails. Grammarly and other add-ons can assist you in improving your writing abilities and clarity. They're especially useful when drafting a report and sending it to your boss through email. If there are many errors, your employer or client may doubt your ability to email professionally. Whether or not you use Grammarly or other add-ons, it's critical to reread your emails. You'll ensure that your email not only makes sense but also has no errors or typos by doing so. To put it another way, read the email from your recipient's perspective and then figure out what needs to be addressed.

Managing Remote Employees Performance Without Seeming Cold and Distant

Here are some tactics suggested based on my experience for how HR departments might encourage the shift to remote performance management:

1. Determine the Various Remote Performance Management Needs

Traditional performance management and remote performance management have significant distinctions. Performance is essentially a measure of achievement against a set of objectives. As a result, it's critical to be explicit about the grounds on which you're basing your evaluation. To do so, consider how your company's goals have shifted since the COVID-19 crisis and the inevitable shift to remote working.

2. Establish clear goals and expectations.

Employees can align their performance when they understand what is expected of them. Understanding the parameters of one's job is one of the most difficult tasks for remote workers. They don't have a clear direction, and they can't study their peers or learn from their bosses, unlike when they work in an office. As a result, it's critical to establish clear expectations and define detailed goals and work descriptions from the start.

3. Keep track of the goals.

It's critical to keep track of whether your staff is consistently fulfilling their objectives once you've set them. You can set weekly goals as part of the broader aim or targets that the company is attempting to achieve and then have employees submit weekly progress reports. You'll be able to see who consistently produces and who falls short.

Task completion tracking tools can be as simple as Google forms and Google sheets or as sophisticated as software like Tasks in Microsoft Teams, HiveDesk, Jira, Time Doctor, etc. If creating reports is too time-consuming, you can schedule frequent status updates. This will encourage team transparency and responsibility and act as a useful reference point for performance reviews.

4. Put Employees in a Position of Trust

Managers may be left wondering about their employees' daily schedules due to their inability to supervise them personally. Managers may feel compelled to micromanage or over-monitor team operations to acquire visibility and control over their personnel. HR can make a difference in this situation by assisting managers in learning about the best team management methods for the remote working environment.

Managers must have faith in their employees and inspire them to perform without imposing excessive pressure or control. Giving employees more autonomy and flexibility as long as they complete tasks on time is a powerful show of trust that they will notice and appreciate.

5. Use technology to manage remote performance.

With the development of remote working, a flood of tools and software to help manage remote employee performance has flooded the market. You need visibility into what your employees are doing to maximize their efficiency while telecommuting and supporting your team. Without being intrusive or disturbing, the greatest automatic programmes provide exactly that. Trello, Slack, Timely, and other crucial remote employee management applications included.

Make sure the performance management tools you're using don't add to your team's workload. They should be as basic and intuitive to use as possible, and they should only perform one thing well. Check out for companies that use artificial intelligence (AI) and automation to reduce duplication of labor.

6. Understand that performance varies from one employee to another.

It's not easy to transition to a remote work environment. With the flexible work arrangement, you should also be flexible and sympathetic with your staff regarding performance management. It's critical to give employees a little more leeway while adjusting to remote work and balancing their personal lives. You shouldn't just focus on the deliverables; you should also assist them in adapting to change.

With this in mind, it's preferable to make performance evaluations more subjective by using a flexible performance rating system that accounts for the challenges that employees confront when they migrate to remote work. Instead of clear ratings or rankings, a narrative assessment that recognizes the employee's efforts while also providing precise advice about their improvement is recommended.

7. Collect several types of performance data

The fact that you don't have much data to work with is one of the most difficult parts of doing performance reviews remotely. Past experiences and inherent biases may also have an impact on the evaluation process. It's critical to examine other data sources while dealing with such problems. Self-evaluations, peer evaluations, and manager evaluations, for example, can all be useful data points. Training costs, income per employee, time to completion rate, and other factors can all be considered.

8. Frequent Performance Conversations are necessary.

Due to intense work pressure or hectic schedules, it may be tempting for managers to postpone or even cancel performance conversations. Performance discussions, on the other hand, should not be isolated or one-time events. HR should make it essential for managers to have to continue performance dialogues with employees to make course corrections at their own pace rather than waiting until the end of the year when it is too late.

9. Dealing with Non-Achievers

Performance evaluations are a fantastic opportunity for managers to directly connect with non-performers and discuss strategies to improve in a normal work environment. However, in a remote work environment, you cannot be as demanding and pursue non-performers. Take the time to engage them in a dialogue to learn what limits them from providing their best.

Perhaps the employee will require some time to become accustomed to the remote working equipment. If that's the case, offer underperforming staff a little more time to improve. Also, make sure you provide adequate development coaching to assist them in developing abilities that they may need to accomplish their work.

10. Recognize and reward outstanding performers

On the other hand, make sure that top achievers are recognized for their contributions. This will significantly raise staff morale and your company's ability to retain top talent. So, take advantage of this opportunity to show your thanks to your staff and promote a positive work environment.

11. Dealing with Online Harassment

While performance is crucial, organizations often overlook the importance of behavior. You can be tempted to believe that there are no dangers of unacceptable behavior such as bullying or invading someone's personal space because there are no in-person encounters. The truth is rather different. Virtual harassment is increasing, and it needs to be addressed. To address misconduct and virtual harassment incidents in the remote workplace, organizations should establish the appropriate decorum and raise awareness.

12. Take a look ahead

As companies shift to remote performance management, it's critical to think long-term and adjust your strategy accordingly. In a remote workplace, regular performance reviews, such as quarterly or monthly check-ins, are required.

These types of evaluations provide the way for open and honest feedback, which employees appreciate. It also enables them to make immediate adjustments to their performance. With this in mind, come up with the best remote performance management solutions from a futuristic standpoint.

Tips to Run Effective Brainstorming Sessions Remotely

A brainstorming session aids teams in generating crazy and imaginative ideas for the future of our products. It can also assist participants in taking a step back from a difficult situation and charting a course ahead. Whether you're brainstorming something as detailed as what features a product you're building must have, something as strategic as to how to create more inclusive working environments to a remote-only setup, brainstorms can help.

However, because many of us will be working from home for the foreseeable future, the traditional brainstorming structure will need to be adjusted. We no longer have the luxury of brainstorming ideas together in a room, whiteboarding side by side, or collecting ideas on sticky notes and mapping them out in real-time. Unfortunately, when brainstorming goes virtual, it's all too easy to tune out, whether due to distractions in your local environment (hello, infants, pets, husbands, and grandparents!) or just because you're (understandably) Zoom-fatigued.

Fortunately, brainstorming is particularly adaptive to a remote setting. We can maintain some of the basic building elements of a live brainstorm in place while adding the required "twist" to keep things exciting and video-call friendly.

Here are seven strategies for conducting a productive video conference brainstorming session:

Get the Scope Right

You'll need to explicitly define your scope, just as you would for an in-person brainstorm. To do so, make certain you can:

Describe the situation. Why?

Why are we having this brainstorm now? What is your planned outcome, and what is your goal? Ensure that this is a matter that merits numerous voices in the same room as a good gut check. So, consider this: Is this a nuanced discussion? Will you need to enlist the help of stakeholders? Are you trying to come up with a list of actionable next steps? If you answered no to any of these questions, you risk wasting other people's time on something that might have been accomplished by email or asynchronously. Remote brainstorming is especially useful for thorny topics that are difficult to articulate in an email thread (e.g., conversations about inclusion), challenges that require alignment (e.g., getting several executives in one room to debate an issue instead of getting input one by one), and projects that are stuck and require action (such as deciding on a set of features to build next). On the other hand, a brainstorm may not be the ideal choice if you're seeking a simple thumb up or thumbs down or plain input to continue forward. Knowing what you want to get out of the brainstorm (a decision, a list of ideas to try, etc.) will help you design it afterward.

Carefully select your participants.

Stick to the essentials—a bloated brainstorm can be a pain to manage, especially over video chat, because the more people who chime in, the more individuals are mistakenly stopped, the more points are repeated, and the more time is lost. ("Excuse me, but what did you say?") "Oops, you get to go first!" Okay, how about I take the lead? Sorry, but you get to go first!") Consider when you'll need input from specific people, such as decision-makers, influencers, or subject matter experts, when making your shortlist.

1 – Keep it brief

Keep it to an hour or less—any longer, and individuals will become bored, distracted, or drop off to attend to competing priorities. Whether you have a topic that is too big for an hour, this is your chance to brutally prioritize and reconsider whether everything needs to be discussed in a group or if some of it can be delegated to asynchronous channels. If a topic is absolutely critical to discuss as a group and an hour won't suffice, consider holding numerous brainstorming sessions over a few days to get it done, but this should only be used as a last resort.

2. Prepare Your Audience

If you want to be sure that your participants have enough knowledge to be helpful in the meeting, whether you have a brainstorm in person or online. Tell them ahead of time what you anticipate of them so they can prepare and arrive on time to make the most of your time together. This could contain things like the session's flow, the brainstorm's goals, and the role you're hoping they'll play.

I also recommend giving participants a heads-up on what tools or resources they'll need, especially remote sessions. So, if you're going to use Google Slides, make sure everyone has an account. If you're going to introduce a new tool, have them set it up ahead of time. You might consider assigning pre-work using the same tools you'll use during your session to ensure that everyone has access to the documents and resources you'll use and can navigate them independently.

3. Keep Them Engaged

When it's time for your meeting, adhere to your schedule and make every effort to keep things going. To overcome the distance imposed by screens, you'll need to provide extra excitement! Ask participants to turn on their webcams and turn off their microphones until they speak; this will let everyone feel like they are part of a shared experience without causing extra disruption. Like Zoom and Google Meet, many video conferencing systems provide gallery and grid views that allow you to see all participants at once, which can help you assess where energy is waning and keep the entire group interested.

Additionally, you'll want to keep things lively. Assign various tasks to group members so that everyone is involved in the game. For example, ask someone to assist you with note-taking, someone else to assist you with any technical issues, and someone else to serve as a timekeeper. (Just make sure the same people don't get the same "housework" responsibilities every time.) This allows you to conduct the session more efficiently while still keeping others occupied.

Finally, "planting" an ally or two to help break the ice and start the dialogue is a good idea. Remember that the energy in the "room" is different when we're remote, so encouraging a few teammates to lead the way and model strong engagement from the start might be beneficial.

4. Make Collaboration Simple for Others

Prepare a screen with brainstorming prompts for everyone to use as needed, for example. You can share the document with the people participating and use page numbers to direct them to what you want them to focus on at any particular time if you don't want to leave it up for the entire time because you want everyone to see each other's faces. Instead of staying in one large group the entire time, consider creating breakout groups to explore prompts and develop ideas. If you go this path, you'll need to choose a facilitator for each "room" to keep track of the dialogue and ideas that emerge.

5. Use digital tools to collect data

It is not necessary to employ fancy tools for brainstorming sessions. Figma, a brainstorming tool, is one option, while Google Sheets is another. Participants can post ideas, vote on ideas (emojis are wonderful for this), similar group ideas, and more using digital tools. The most crucial aspect is sharing your screen or file with others and having everyone be able to edit at the same time to add their suggestions.

Prep your document ahead of time by designating each participant a dedicated location to scribble down their comments, whether it's a row in Excel, a set of digital post-its in Figma, or their own slide in Google Slides. The goal is to keep everyone's cursors from interfering with each other.

Have No Fear, Remote Work Is Here!

6. Do not attempt to live-synthesize

Of course, you'll eventually want to make sense of everyone's contributions and begin grouping their ideas so that they may be implemented. This strategy works well in person, but it can feel like a waste of time on film. Instead, pay attention to any patterns or trends you notice, but keep the in-depth analysis for when you're alone. Depending on your workplace culture, communicate the results in a wrap-up doc, deck, or even a Slack message. It will save a lot of time.

7. Concluding

As your time together comes to an end, there are a few basic measures you may take to wrap things up. For example, before you leave, ask participants to email over any assets or ideas that were not captured in your shared doc so that they can be included in your synthesis process. As a group, finalize future steps and assign owners for responsibility.

Send a brief summary of what you learned after the session, and don't forget to thank your colleagues for attending. These days, it takes a lot of days to develop ideas, especially remotely; therefore, everyone deserves a standing ovation. You may also want to seek feedback on how things went, especially if this was your first remote brainstorm—always there's an opportunity for better!

What are Some of the Best Places Where Employees Can Go to Work?

The appeal of remote employment is its flexibility. You may simply pack up and work from a different location if you get tired of your home office. Variety is a terrific motivator, as it breaks up your workweek and provides much-needed social interaction. Finding the proper remote workstation, on the other hand, is an art. Here's my list of the greatest locations to work remotely from home to help you find your ideal home office.

1. Quiet cafes

Take note of the word "quiet": while cafés provide warm, pleasant, caffeine-rich environments, they are also rife with distractions. Because these are community places, expect to work in an environment with a lot of noise and constant chatter (which can be parallel with nightclubs). Many cafes offer free Wi-Fi and plug sockets, while others do not; always check to see if a workspace precedent has been established before you settle there.

2. Galleries and museums

Museums are a fascinating contrast to your office since they are calm, quiet, and nearly always housed in great buildings. In-house eateries usually have plenty of seating and food options, and you may utilize your break time to learn something new.

3. Public libraries

You should join your local library if you haven't already done so because they're fantastic. They also make for quite effective remote workstations, aside from helping your community. They're best employed for intense, distraction-free deep work. (Printing capabilities are a plus.)

4. Bookstores

Few things will drive you to focus on your work more than a comfortable, bookish environment. More booksellers include quiet places and cafes into their offerings, combining the benefits of café culture with the convenience of a library.

5. Collaborative workspaces

Consider joining a local co-working space if you need a little more structure in your workspace. They effectively serve as a second office away from home, with all of the necessary office equipment and refreshment and, in some cases, leisure facilities. With a focus on friendly working, there's plenty of chances to meet new people, network, and share ideas.

6. Arts and cultural institutions

Art centers with a similar ambiance to museums and galleries provide a more inspired remote work area with all the bells and whistles. Look into performing arts centers in your area, such as the Barbican in London and the Oslo Opera House. Putting yourself in a creative setting is a terrific approach to boost your creative abilities.

7. College and university spaces

Although some regions may require an access card, university campuses offer various options for productive remote work. It's what they were made for, so expect to see them in a variety of indoor and outdoor settings. If you find the student's company motivating rather than distracting, it's worth a shot.

8. Private member clubs

There are fewer of these professional members clubs nowadays, but they are useful havens for effective remote work. They effectively serve the same purpose as co-working spaces but with a more upscale feel. Many offer corporate events and conferences regularly, making them excellent learning environments.

9. Historic sites

You might find a few unusual cultural locations in your neighborhood that you've never considered working in before. Historic estates, botanical gardens, theatres, and even castles are fantastic options for seats and drinks. The novelty boosts your motivation, and you get a kick out of discovering new places while you work.

10. Department stores

Have No Fear, Remote Work Is Here!

Like your local café, department shops have their drawbacks, but they can be a fantastic place to work remotely if you can get past the noise and distractions. Top floors are nearly generally allocated for eateries and cafés, providing various workspaces and a good view.

11. A separate residence

Let's face it; nothing compares to the comfort and tranquility of one's own home. So, if you're tired of working from your own home office, try working from a different location! Consider creating a "home office rotation" schedule with other remote worker buddies to keep things fresh.

My final request…

Being a smaller author, reviews help me tremendously!

It would mean the world to me if you could leave a review.

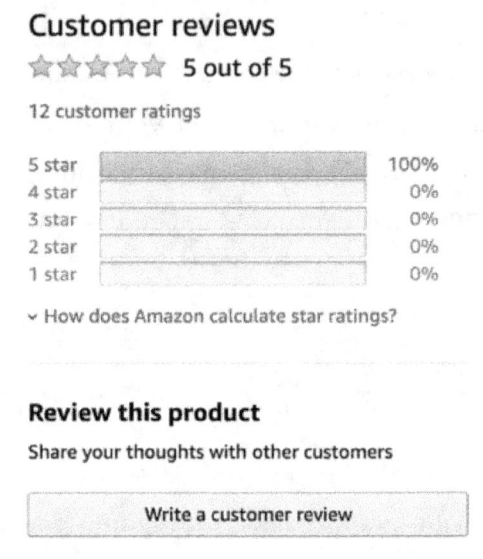

If you liked reading this book and learned a thing or two, please let me know!

It only takes 30 seconds but means so much to me!

CONCLUSION

This book was written with the sole purpose of assisting you in your remote work journey as it is being considered the future of employment. I tried my best to cover everything that I had been through while I was on my journey of remote work. The data and statistics provided to you have been written keeping in mind the problems and hurdles that I had to face. I can assure you that everything written in this book isn't just theory but practically applicable for every common man working remotely. The strategies that have been discussed in this book are what I end up framing personally, and a few of them have been taken after keen research over various companies and employees that have been working remotely and got help from these tactics and techniques in order to run the flow of remote work smoothly.

This book included everything from actual remote work to how any employer or employee can practice it effectively. You can eliminate your commute, work where you focus best, and spend more time doing things you enjoy while developing your career when you harness the potential of remote work. This book demonstrated how to use today's cloud-based communication and collaboration tools to do tasks from any location while remaining connected to your firm. It also highlighted how you could establish a productive work environment at home or in the office by properly planning your day and eliminating distractions. Also, how to establish rapport with remote coworkers so that you feel like a member of the team and succeed in your distant job. I am confident that this would have aided you in the most effective way possible in learning how to work

Have No Fear, Remote Work Is Here!

successfully when and where you desire and achieve the freedom and flexibility you require for a more balanced existence.

To summarize, this book describes the ideal home setup for working remotely, summarizes the process of onboarding a remote worker, explains the importance of work-life balance and how to maintain it while working remotely, cites the tools remote workers can use to stay connected to the home office and explains how to maintain it while working remotely.

I hope you've enjoyed reading it and have learned a lot.

Resources

1. Davies, N., n.d. *Want To Work Remotely? Here's How To Convince Your Boss*. [online] Forbes. Available at: <https://www.forbes.com/sites/nigeldavies/2020/02/19/want-to-work-remotely-heres-how-to-convince-your-boss/?sh=2ff351ff4c56>.

2. Medium. n.d. *Why You Shouldn't Pay Remote Workers Based on Where They Live*. [online] Available at: <https://marker.medium.com/why-you-shouldnt-pay-remote-workers-based-on-where-they-live-bc151b616048#_=_>.

3. Forbes. n.d. *Council Post: Four Metrics That Matter For Remote Workers*. [online] Available at: <https://www.forbes.com/sites/theyec/2020/08/24/four-metrics-that-matter-for-remote-workers/?sh=15e555777e40>.

4. NH Business Review. n.d. *Adjusting to a new reality - NH Business Review*. [online] Available at: <https://www.nhbr.com/adjusting-to-a-new-reality/>.

5. [online] Available at: <https://www.mckinsey.com/featured-insights/future-of-work/whats-next-for-remote-work-an-analysis-of-2000-tasks-800-jobs-and-nine-countries>.

6. Murphy, M., n.d. *6 Traits Of Leaders Who Successfully Manage Remote Employees*. [online] Forbes. Available at: <https://www.forbes.com/sites/markmurphy/2016/06/10/6-traits-of-leaders-who-successfully-manage-remote-employees/?sh=1f06fb424032>.

7. Harvard Business Review. n.d. *Remote Managers Are Having Trust Issues*. [online] Available at: <https://hbr.org/2020/07/remote-managers-are-having-trust-issues>.

8. Uc.com.co. n.d. [online] Available at: <https://uc.com.co/wp-content/uploads/2020/03/A-blueprint-for-remote-working-Lessons-from-China-vF.pdf>.

9. Cohen, A., n.d. *The surprising traits of good remote leaders.* [online] Bbc.com. Available at: <https://www.bbc.com/worklife/article/20200827-why-in-person-leaders-may-not-be-the-best-virtual-ones>.

10. Harvard Business Review. n.d. *How to Tell Someone They're Being Laid Off.* [online] Available at: <https://hbr.org/2015/06/how-to-tell-someone-theyre-being-laid-off>.

11. Alexander, A., De Smet, A., Langstaff, M., & Ravid, D. (2021). *What employees are saying about the future of remote work.* Mckinsey.com. https://www.mckinsey.com/business-functions/organization/our-insights/what-employees-are-saying-about-the-future-of-remote-work.

www.ingramcontent.com/pod-product-compliance
Lightning Source LLC
LaVergne TN
LVHW012041070526
838202LV00056B/5556